New Friends at the Ballet School

Mal Lewis Jones

Hodder
Children's
Books

a division of Hodder Headline plc

Children for cover illustration by courtesy of Gaston Payne
School of Theatre, Dance and Drama.

Special thanks to Freed of London Ltd., 94 St Martins Lane,
London WC2N for the loan of dancewear.

First published in Great Britain in 1994
by Hodder Children's Books

A Catalogue record for this book is available from the British Library

ISBN 0 340 60731 9

Typeset by Avon Dataset Ltd, Bidford-on-Avon

Printed and bound in Great Britain by
Cox & Wyman Ltd, Reading, Berks.

Hodder Children's Books
A Division of Hodder Headline plc
338 Euston Road
London NW1 3BH

Contents

For my daughter, Lara

1

A New Housemother

Cassie Brown picked one of the lighter bags from the boot of the car, tossed her long, curly, brown hair over her shoulder and flew across the entrance drive, leaving her Dad, Jake, to follow rather more slowly with her suitcases. There were cars, kids and parents everywhere. The first day of the school year at Redwood Ballet School was always like this. Cassie already felt like an old hand, even though it was only the beginning of her second year.

She was soon chattering excitedly to her friend Emily Pickering, whom she hadn't seen since the previous term. Emily particularly wanted to know how their friend Becky was. Becky had been very ill with meningitis at the end of last term, and it had seemed likely that she would have to leave Redwood.

'She's getting on really well,' said Cassie happily. 'We had a great time when she came to stay with me.'

'That's good,' said Emily. 'I was so relieved when you wrote to me that she was coming back to school. Redwood just wouldn't have been the same without Becky.'

'The only problem she's still got is with her balance.'

'Mmm, not too good for pirouettes. Where is she anyway?' asked Emily, looking round at the milling students.

'Oh, didn't I tell you? Her parents have taken her on holiday to Crete. She's going to miss the first week of term.'

'Lucky thing!' cried Emily. A sad expression flitted across her face. 'My mum could do with a holiday, if anyone could. She looks worn out.'

Cassie squeezed her friend's shoulder. She knew what a struggle Mrs Pickering was having, bringing up five children single-handed.

Emily sighed. 'I don't know what I'm going to do for equipment this year. The bursary's all used up now, and I've grown out of all my leotards and dancing shoes over the summer.'

'Same here,' said Cassie. 'But don't worry, I'm sure they'll give you the Allingham bursary again. And in the meantime, I've got spare leotards you can borrow.'

As Emily looked into Cassie's warm, brown eyes, a smile lit up her pale face. 'It's lovely to be back with you, Cassie.'

The girls joined their respective parents in the entrance hall and jostled their way through the crush by the notice-boards, trying to read the room allocations.

'Cross your fingers Miss Eiseldown has put us together!' shouted Cassie, above the racket.

'We're both in Room Twelve,' said Emily, after catching a glimpse of the board. 'And Becky too!'

'Brilliant!'

'Come on, Emily, let's take your stuff up to your room,' said Emily's mother. 'I haven't much time.'

Cassie could see what Emily meant about her mother looking worn out. Mrs Pickering was just like her daughter in build – petite and nimble in her movements. But her face had grown haggard and careworn.

As they began to move out of the hall, Cassie rescued her dad, who was looking hot and flustered, and showed him the way to Room Twelve. It was on the same landing as their old room, but was larger. The deep sash window overlooked the drive and grounds at the front of the building. Mrs Pickering put all Emily's bags on her bed.

'I'll have to leave you, love, I'm afraid,' she said. 'Got to get back for the children,' she explained to Jake. She gave Emily a quick hug and was gone.

Jake admired the view while Cassie unpacked. 'Those redwood trees are a tremendous height!' he exclaimed.

'Who else is sharing with us?' Cassie asked Emily. 'There are five beds. We'll bags this one next to us for Becky.'

'I didn't recognise the other two names, but one looked Japanese. They must be new girls.'

'Well, cross your fingers again, Emily – that they're OK, I mean.'

'Shh, you two,' warned Jake, who had spotted someone approaching their room. A beautiful Japanese girl walked in, followed by her parents – a good-looking Japanese man and a pretty, fair-haired English woman. This combination of parents had produced an extremely striking child. She looked oriental, with dark eyes and glossy, black hair, but had an English bloom to her skin and a rose-bud mouth.

The couple introduced themselves and their daughter to Jake and the girls. Their surname was Fujiwara, and the girl's name was Mitsuko.

As the adults fell into conversation, Cassie and Emily couldn't take their eyes off Mitsuko. They had never seen such long hair, for a start. She wore it loose and Cassie guessed she could easily sit on it. Realising she was being rude – staring at Mitsuko as she was – Cassie started pointing out which drawers, desk and bit of the wardrobe the new girl could use, and where the bathroom was. It was all quite obvious really, but it was something to break the ice.

All too soon it was time to say goodbye to her dad. She remembered the same moment twelve months ago – how terribly nervous she had felt. There was still a pang as she had to let him go this time. She noticed Mitsuko clinging to her mother as they parted and thought how much worse it must be for her,

4

knowing her parents were flying back to Japan.

'Give us a ring on Tuesday, darling,' said Jake cheerfully. 'And don't fall out with Miss Wrench again!' He winked at her as he left the room. Cassie laughed, but the reminder of the awful few weeks at the end of last term, when she had been accused of stealing, made her shiver inwardly. She shook herself, as if to free her mind from those black memories. Everything was all right now. The true culprit had been found, and Cassie had been cleared of all suspicion.

The door opened and their other new room-mate bustled in, loaded with baggage. She was red-haired, freckle-faced and athletic-looking.

'Hi, I'm Poppy!' she said brightly, dumping everything in a heap on the empty bed. The others looked expectantly at the door, but no parent followed. Poppy guessed their train of thought.

'Oh, I'm on my own. Australia's a long way!'

'So is Japan,' said Mitsuko, rather tearfully. She spoke perfect English, even though she had been living in Tokyo for the last six years.

'I'm Cassie,' said Cassie, grinning. 'And this is Mitsuko and Emily.'

'Will I like it here?' asked Poppy, sprawling on top of her bags. By contrast, Mitsuko perched gingerly on the edge of her bed; her possessions had already been put away neatly.

'I'm sure you will,' said Cassie enthusiastically. 'If you like ballet, that is.'

'That goes without saying, doesn't it?'

5

'Well . . . not always,' said Cassie, thinking of her animal-loving friend, Becky.

'*I* don't like it all that much,' confessed Mitsuko.

'What?' exclaimed Cassie. 'Why have you come all this way then?'

Mitsuko shrugged. 'My mother has always wanted me to be educated in England, and she knows I'm good at dancing.' Her voice caught in a suppressed sob.

'Come on, everybody,' said Cassie, shooting to her feet. 'Supper-time.'

'Oh great,' said Poppy. 'Lunch on the plane seems years ago. I'm starving.'

'I'm not very hungry,' said Mitsuko, looking miserable. Cassie pulled her gently to her feet. 'Well, come and talk to us anyway,' she said.

But before they had a chance to leave the bedroom, the door opened and a large woman walked in. She had a haircut which looked like the bristles of a nailbrush, unflattering clothes and tiny, but piercing, blue eyes.

'Good evening,' she said. 'My name's Mrs Ramsbottom. I'm your new housemother.'

Cassie and Emily exchanged shocked looks. What had happened to Miss Eiseldown?

'Just thought I'd introduce myself and let you know how I expect you to behave in this house.'

Mrs Ramsbottom paused and looked meaningfully at Poppy's bed, still untidily strewn with her belongings.

'There will be an inspection of your room every morning, to see that beds have been made, rugs

6

shaken, etc. I expect everything to be ship-shape. Uniform and equipment will be inspected weekly. They'd better be spotless, or I'll want to know why!'

Mrs Ramsbottom was beginning to bark out her instructions like a sergeant-major. Cassie couldn't believe this awful woman was a replacement for their lovely Miss Eiseldown.

'Now, which of you are Cassandra and Emily?'

Cassie and Emily introduced themselves.

'Right, girls. You are to take responsibility for the first-year group in the room opposite. Is that understood?'

'Yes, Mrs Ramsbottom.'

'Don't forget. Lights out at eight-thirty, on the dot. Good evening.'

'Good evening, Mrs Ramsbottom.'

As the door closed, Cassie put her back against it and pretended to wipe the sweat from her brow with the back of her hand.

'I don't believe this,' she said.

'Where on earth is Miss Eiseldown?' Emily asked. But no answer was forthcoming, when they asked fellow students at supper.

In the dining-hall Mitsuko looked more miserable than ever and Cassie found it hard work bringing her into the conversation with their old friends, Matthew and Tom. The boys enjoyed Cassie's impersonation of Mrs Ramsbottom, and by the end of it, even Mitsuko had managed a weak smile.

'She must have taught at a very strict school before this,' suggested Matthew.

'She's probably got a heart of gold underneath,' said Tom.

Cassie laughed derisively, exposing the generous gap between her top front teeth.

'Oh, I wish Miss Eiseldown were still here,' said Emily.

'It won't be too bad,' said Poppy cheerfully. 'We'll only see her in the morning, I guess. Then we can forget about her for the rest of the day. Who's coming up for seconds?'

'Oh, not me, thanks,' groaned Cassie, patting her over-full stomach. 'Have you finished, Emily? I thought we'd pay our first years a visit.'

'Good idea.'

It made the two girls feel quite grown up, having younger ones to look after. Cassie called into her own room first to pick up several soft toys, which she intended to lend the first years. They slipped across the landing to the room opposite and knocked. The three younger girls were all back from supper, and glad to see friendly faces.

'Hi! You found your way to the dining-hall and back all right then?'

Cassie glanced round the room. It hadn't changed much since she shared it with Becky and Amanda last year. She remembered the good times with Becky – the tricks, the midnight feasts – and then the rows with Amanda. It all seemed a long time ago.

Two of the first years looked tearful, and Cassie's cuddly toys came in useful. The third girl, Lesley, seemed to be covering up her nervousness by being loud and boisterous. Jumping on her bed, she started singing a pop song at the top of her voice.

'I shouldn't be too noisy, if I . . .' Emily began.

Mrs Ramsbottom's voice cut across Emily's like a scythe. She stood, arms folded, in the doorway. 'And just *who* is making my hair stand on end?'

Cassie could see that Lesley's courage had deserted her, and felt sorry that she was going to get into trouble on her very first evening. Without thinking of the consequences, Cassie stepped forward, her chin jutting out slightly.

'It was me, Mrs Ramsbottom,' she said. 'I'm sorry.'

'Cassandra, isn't it? And you're a second year?'

'Yes.'

'I'm most surprised. That's hardly setting a good example to the first years. You'd better have a black mark.'

'Yes, Mrs Ramsbottom.'

When the housemother had gone, they settled the first years down for the night. 'Thank you, Cassandra,' said Lesley, 'for saving my skin!'

Cassie shrugged and followed Emily out on to the landing.

'Whatever made you do that?' asked Emily.

'I just felt sorry for Lesley, that's all,' said Cassie. 'But I've a horrible feeling that Mrs Ramsbottom is not going to like me much from now on.'

Cassie and Emily returned to their own room to find Mitsuko huddled under her duvet, sobbing quietly.

'Oh Mitsi! Can I call you that?' said Emily gently.

9

'Don't cry. You'll feel so much better by tomorrow, believe me.'

Cassie offered Mitsi her teddy and Mitsi snuggled down with it gratefully.

'What time do we get up?' asked Poppy, when she came in from doing her exercises.

'Just before seven. Breakfast at half-past,' said Cassie, slipping into her pyjamas.

'I think I *am* going to like it here,' said Poppy. 'Everyone's so friendly.'

'With one or two exceptions!' laughed Cassie, thinking of Mrs Ramsbottom.

Poppy nodded and a huge grin spread over her freckled face. Cassie suddenly realised why she was called Poppy – her bright red hair!

'Have you been dancing long?' Cassie asked her.

'Since I was three. How about you?'

'Oh, I was much older when I started – seven. But Australia's so far away. Haven't you got ballet schools over there you could go to?'

'Yes, of course we have. I went to an academy for a year; then I won a bursary to transfer here, and my teacher advised me to come.'

'Well, Redwood's certainly the best in this country,' said Cassie.

'It's half-past eight, you two,' Emily interrupted. 'I'm switching off the light.'

'Well done, Em,' said Cassie. 'It's a good job I've got you to keep me in order.'

2

The Haircut

Cassie was woken the next morning by a horrifying
noise. Someone was marching along the landing,
hammering on people's doors and yelling, 'Chop,
chop. Rise and shine!'

Still in a stupor, Cassie tumbled out of bed and
caught sight of Mitsi's white face.

'Don't worry, Mitsi. It's only Mrs Ramsbottom.'

'Miss Eiseldown always used to come into the rooms
and wake you gently, if you weren't already awake,'
said Emily sadly.

'I don't think Mrs Ramsbottom could do anything
gently,' added Cassie.

'Can't someone shut that woman up?' moaned

Poppy, pulling her pillow over her ears.

'Are you very tired?' asked Emily.

'I didn't sleep well,' answered Poppy.

'Nor me,' said Mitsi. 'I tossed and turned all night long. I just wanted to be back in my own bed.'

'It'll get better,' promised Cassie. 'Now, let me show you how to do your hair. They're very fussy here about having it just so.'

'I'll pop across to give the first years a hand,' said Emily.

'Well, watch out for Lesley,' warned Cassie. 'If she starts getting noisy again, shut her up quick.'

'Yes, I will,' laughed Emily, leaving the room.

Cassie started brushing Mitsi's glossy, waist-length hair. But after she had made two plaits, she found it very difficult to wind them round Mitsi's head – they were so thick and long.

As she was struggling to pin them in place, Mrs Ramsbottom walked in to inspect the room.

'Where are Poppy and Emily?' she demanded.

'Emily's helping the first years and Poppy's in the bathroom, Mrs Ramsbottom,' Cassie said.

'This room is nowhere near ready. Poppy's bed is still unmade! It's a disgrace!'

Then she caught sight of Mitsi's hair.

'Don't you know the regulations, Mitsuko?' she said, turning on the quaking girl. 'Hair is to be shoulder-length, neither shorter, nor longer. Cassandra, you must take Mitsuko to Matron before breakfast to get it cut. You can't do anything with it like that!'

'Yes, Mrs Ramsbottom,' answered Cassie, thinking

privately that this was going to upset Mitsi terribly. Sure enough, Mitsi burst into tears just as Poppy came back into the room.

Mrs Ramsbottom promptly turned her attention on Poppy, giving her five minutes to tidy her bed and belongings.

'And when I come back,' she warned, 'I expect the rugs to have been shaken. And please put out all your uniform and equipment – ballet or academic – for me to check. We shall have a weekly check on Monday mornings. Is that understood?'

'Yes, Mrs Ramsbottom.' Cassie was the only one to speak. Mitsi was still crying and Poppy was dumbfounded. Discipline had been nothing like this in Australia! For the next five minutes, the girls rushed around like mad things. Emily came back in time to lay out her uniform for checking. When Mrs Ramsbottom returned, everything, at least to their eyes, had been put in order. But Mrs Ramsbottom managed to find some specks of mud on Cassie's outdoor shoes, and told Poppy off for having an untidy locker. She held up one of Emily's leotards and looked at Emily.

'Is this the right size?' she asked.

'I think I may have grown a little in the holidays, Mrs Ramsbottom,' said Emily warily.

Mrs Ramsbottom snorted. 'You should have made sure all your uniform fitted before term started. You've had eight weeks to buy new leotards! So why are you here on the first day of classes without proper equipment?'

13

Emily went very red but made no answer. She was saved from further questioning by a messenger from Miss Wrench.

'Emily Pickering? Could you go to see the Principal immediately, please?'

Cassie breathed a sigh of relief that her friend could escape.

'When you have cleaned your shoes, Cassandra,' was Mrs Ramsbottom's parting shot, 'you can take Mitsuko for her haircut!'

A little later, Cassie took a sobbing Mitsi to Matron's room, and explained to the shy little woman what Mrs Ramsbottom had requested.

Cassie could hardly bear to watch the haircut. She never minded her own hair being trimmed, but she could see how important Mitsi's long hair was to her. Even Matron was terribly apologetic. Cassie had brought a hairbrush and bands and pins with her, so that Matron could plait Mitsi's hair afterwards. Then they quickly went down for breakfast, where Emily and Poppy were waiting for them.

'What did Miss Wrench want?' Cassie asked.

'Oh, good news,' said Emily with a big smile. 'I'm to have the Allingham bursary for this year, and Miss Wrench told me to go straight to the stock cupboard and get what I need.'

'Oh, that's great,' said Cassie. 'I knew you'd be all right.' She glanced across at Mitsi, who hadn't touched her cereal and was still sobbing.

'Poor Mitsi – it must have been heart-breaking seeing her lovely hair lying in heaps on Matron's floor.'

'It's all that stupid Mrs Ramsbottom's fault,' said Emily. 'She should have left her alone until she'd settled in.'

'Oh, whatever's happened to Miss Eiseldown?' asked Cassie. 'She didn't mention she was leaving.'

'Perhaps she's got married?' suggested Emily.

'But that still doesn't explain why she left,' retorted Cassie.

By the time ballet class had begun, Cassie was relieved to see Mitsi had managed to compose herself. Disappointingly, their ballet mistress for the term was to be Miss Oakland and not Madame Larette, everyone's favourite. However, it was good to be working hard again and Cassie enjoyed stretching out the stiffness in her muscles. Even though she had done daily practice at home, you could never really push yourself as hard as a teacher could.

It was interesting, too, to look round at the new girls. Mitsi was coping, but with a bit of a struggle, whereas Poppy was obviously a very capable dancer, who could adapt to a new style very easily. There were four other new ones, the most striking of whom was a black girl called Abigail, who was also a very strong dancer. Cassie's heart sank a little. With her old rival Amanda out of the way, she had hoped to be best in the class. But it looked as if she had competition again! At least Poppy was nice, though. She would have to wait and see about Abigail.

After their curtsy at the end of the lesson, Miss Oakland asked the girls to sit down for a few moments, as she had something important to tell them.

'We don't often get opportunities for the Juniors to work professionally, but this season, we're lucky enough to have been asked by the Birmingham Royal Ballet to supply some second and third year girls to audition for the "Dance of the Little Swans".'

A ripple of fidgeting broke out in the room.

'I haven't been given a date as yet, but Madame Larette will be able to tell you a little more when you see her next Thursday for your pointe-work class. Off you go now and don't get too excited – there are only four parts available to your year.'

'Trust Miss Oakland to put the dampers on!' said Cassie in the changing-room later. But, no dampening of spirits was in evidence. The room was vibrant with excitement.

'Oh, wouldn't it be lovely,' said Emily dreamily.

'Sounds a bit soppy to me,' said Poppy, 'but I've never seen *Swan Lake*, so I don't know what the little swans have to do.'

'Oh, it's a gorgeous dance,' said Cassie, grabbing Emily's hand, to try and demonstrate the first few steps to Poppy. She promptly trod on Emily's foot and Poppy burst out laughing.

'Looks more like the "Dance of the Little Elephants" to me,' she spluttered.

Cassie went quiet. She couldn't bear people to laugh at her. She noticed that at the other side of the changing-room, the new girl, Abigail, had a circle of girls round her. She was obviously going to be very popular. Cassie had a sudden longing for Becky to come back, but next week still seemed a long way off.

She turned round to speak to Emily, who was busy helping Mitsuko fasten her grey kilt correctly. Cassie's eyes met Poppy's.

'I was only kidding you,' said Poppy, with a grin. 'I know you're a great dancer really.'

Cassie smiled back. 'Come on then,' she said. 'I'll show you the way to our form-room.'

During form period, the children started to go out one by one for their medicals. This was a termly event, and was taken very seriously by the staff. As Cassie was near the top of the register, she was called out before the end of the period.

'See you at break,' she whispered to Emily. Making her way to the sick-bay area, she shuddered at the thought of stripping down to her regulation school knickers. It would be cold *and* embarrassing, with all those eyes on her. She went into the small waiting-room, and after she'd undressed the nurse weighed and measured her.

'You've shot up!' said the nurse, consulting Cassie's records. 'You've grown three and a half centimetres since last term!'

Groaning inwardly, Cassie wondered if she'd keep growing at this rate for long. Wouldn't it be awful if she ended up too tall! There was no hope of becoming a dancer if you were taller than 1.7 metres or so.

The nurse ushered her into the medical room where the doctor – an orthopaedic consultant – stood waiting by a high bed.

'Good morning, Cassandra,' he said cheerfully. 'Jump up on here, will you please?'

Cassie didn't mind being examined by the doctor, but what was so off-putting was the audience of teachers who sat in a semi-circle behind the bed. Her eyes flicked shyly across the faces. Every single member of the ballet staff was there, including Miss Wrench. She was surprised that they hadn't anything better to do!

As the doctor manipulated her spine and moved her legs in their hip-sockets, Cassie started to feel rather like a performing animal in a circus. After a while, she forgot that it was *her* body they were so interested in, and went off into a daydream. In her mind's eye she was dancing in *Swan Lake*, not as one of the little swans, either, but in the leading role – the swan-princess, Odette.

The doctor's voice startled her when he told her he'd finished, and wished her good morning. She ran off to find Emily in the grounds, conscious that she wouldn't be bumping into any of the ballet staff. The academic staff weren't so strict about moving about the school with decorum, and they didn't expect you to curtsy to them, either. She caught up with Emily at last by the netball court.

'How did you get on?' asked Emily.

'Fine,' puffed Cassie. 'Except I'm growing too much.'

'Lucky you to have your examination over. I'll have to wait all day for mine.'

The bell went and Cassie accompanied Emily, Poppy and Mitsuko to the hall for Junior assembly.

When all the first and second years had gathered,

Miss Wrench entered and mounted the rostrum. She always dressed severely and today was no exception; she was wearing a dark grey suit and all her hair was brushed back off her face and twisted into a French plait. Welcoming the first years and the new second years, she promised them hard but rewarding work at the ballet school, and let them know the most important rules of conduct. Cassie recognised the speech from her own first day the year before. Her mind switched off and once more she was dancing in *Swan Lake*, this time as the counterfeit Odette – the evil Odile.

When she came to, everyone round her was standing up, ready to sing the first hymn. She scrambled to her feet, pink with embarrassment. Mrs Ramsbottom was glowering in her direction. Cassie vowed to keep her mind firmly on what was happening, at least until she was safely away from the new housemother.

'House*dragon* would be a better name,' she thought to herself, as she lustily sang the chorus of 'We Plough the Fields and Scatter':

> All good things around us
> Are sent from Heaven above.
> Then thank the Lord, O thank the Lord,
> For aw-aw-all his love.

'Who sends the bad things then?' wondered Cassie, casting a furtive glance in Mrs Ramsbottom's direction. During the notices at the end of assembly, Cassie's ears pricked up.

'No doubt,' said Miss Wrench, 'some of you second years will have noticed a new face among us, and indeed, a familiar face no longer with us. Mrs Ramsbottom is acting housemother for Landing Two of the Junior Girls' Wing, in place of Miss Eiseldown. I'm sure you will give her every assistance. She will also be taking you for mathematics.

'Miss Eiseldown wished her departure to remain secret last term, but now I can reveal that she has gone to the United States, to teach over there.'

'You were wrong about her getting married,' whispered Cassie, nudging Emily in the ribs.

Before Cassie had time to look round, Mrs Ramsbottom had dived in among the rows of children and grabbed her by the arm. She was hauled out to the side, where the staff sat, and told to stand there until the notices had finished. Blushing angrily, Cassie then had to go up on to the rostrum when all the other children had been dismissed, to apologise to the Principal.

'I think Mrs Ramsbottom saw you talking, Cassandra. Is that correct?'

'Yes, Miss Wrench,' replied Cassie, with a quick curtsy. 'I'm very sorry. I was just so surprised about Miss Eiseldown.'

'Well there is *no* excuse for rudeness. And that's what talking in assembly amounts to, isn't it?'

'Yes, Miss Wrench.'

'Another black mark, Cassandra. I notice you have one already. Not a good start to the term, is it?'

As Miss Wrench dismissed her with a steely look,

Cassie wondered if all the unpleasantness from last term *was* over, or if she was still one of Miss Wrench's least favourite pupils.

3

Celia Reed

'It's just our luck to get landed with Mrs Ramsbottom,' Cassie complained. She and her room-mates were making their way from the dining-hall, where they'd just eaten breakfast, to the ballet studio. Their room inspection that morning had resulted in Cassie's getting another black mark (for an untidy desk), which now put her in detention.

'There's a good programme on TV tonight after supper, as well!' she added crossly.

'Never mind,' said Emily. 'They say bad things come in threes. You've had your lot now.'

'For how long?' asked Cassie. 'With Mrs Ramsbottom as our housemother, I'll be lucky if I don't get a black mark every day.'

'She scares me,' Mitsuko piped up. 'And I shall never forgive her!' She stroked her plaits as she spoke.

'Oh, take no notice!' said Poppy. 'Laugh at her behind her back. It'll do you good.'

'I can't see much to laugh at,' replied Mitsi.

'Well, *I* think she's a strange woman. Makes *me* laugh, anyhow!'

Putting down their bags in the changing-room, the girls quickly changed into their ballet shoes, stripped off their red track suits and made their way into the studio.

Miss Oakland gave them a little talk about preparing for major exams. The girls in her group had all passed Grade Five now (Becky was the only one who hadn't) and so their next exam would be Pre-Elementary. They would have to get used to wearing their pointe shoes for many of the exercises, and so Miss Oakland suggested they work the soles back and forth to make them more flexible.

The syllabus for Pre-Elementary seemed quite a lot more difficult than that for Grade Five, Cassie thought, but she enjoyed the challenge and stimulus of the new work. That morning, she didn't day-dream once.

Her favourite new step was temps de fleche, which took everyone a little while to get the hang of. It involved a spring and a développé devant, unfolding the left leg through the right, ending with the left leg extended in front. After a few disasters, most students mastered it, but none so well as Cassie. She was asked to demonstrate to the class. This made up for all the hassle with Mrs Ramsbottom; praise from Miss Oakland was praise indeed.

Mitsuko was not so lucky; her legs kept getting tangled up every time she attempted the step and Miss Oakland soon lost patience with her.

'Anyone would think you'd grown an extra leg!' she yelled. 'You've only got two, Mitsuko. Keep them under control.'

Mitsi, inevitably, burst into tears, but Miss Oakland took not a scrap of notice. She carried on with the lesson, ignoring Mitsi's sobs.

As Cassie and Emily comforted Mitsi the best they could after class, Abigail and some of the other girls came over to commiserate.

'Don't let her get you down,' Abigail advised. 'Be like me! No one and nothing bothers me. I know I'm good and that's all that matters.'

Cassie wasn't sure she liked such a display of self-confidence, or if it was the right thing to say to Mitsi just at this moment. But there was no doubt that Abigail meant well. Which was more than could be said for the next person to speak – Celia Reed.

'But there's a lot of difference between you and Mitsi,' she said to Abigail. 'I mean, you're one of the best in the class, Abi. I couldn't imagine Miss Oakland ever getting her knives out to *you*!'

Cassie bristled silently. Celia was a new girl, like Abigail, but seemed to make herself unpopular wherever she went. The worst thing about her was that she had quickly made herself Mrs Ramsbottom's favourite, and the other girls suspected her of telling the housemother tales about them. Cassie felt cross that she was being so tactless now to Mitsi.

Even after they'd changed and gone along to their next lesson, Mitsi was still crying. A shock was waiting for them all when they walked into the maths room. Mrs Ramsbottom was sitting at the teacher's desk.

'I'd forgotten she was teaching maths,' whispered Cassie.

'Yes, so had I,' said Emily. 'But I suppose she was bound to take Miss Eiseldown's classes as well.'

Their hearts sank as Mrs Ramsbottom settled them into their first maths lesson of the term – rather like a nail is settled into place by a hammer. It did not escape her notice that Mitsuko had been crying and, rather than make allowances for her, she made a point of asking the girl the most difficult questions. Cassie felt herself growing angrier and angrier with the teacher for picking on Mitsi. Almost as though she could read her thoughts, Mrs Ramsbottom asked Cassie the next question – a very tricky one indeed. Maths had long been Cassie's weakest subject; it called for concentration and logic, neither of which were particular qualities of hers. She felt flustered and cross and couldn't clear her mind long enough to work out the problem. While she was struggling with it, Celia Reed put up her hand and Mrs Ramsbottom invited her to answer.

'Ten thousand and eighty, Mrs Ramsbottom,' said Celia.

'Quite right,' said Mrs Ramsbottom. 'Thank you,

Celia. I'm glad to see *you* are not asleep.'

As Mrs Ramsbottom turned to the blackboard, Celia gave Cassie a smug smile, which Cassie pretended not to notice, but by the time the lunch bell rang, Cassie was seething. She contained herself until she had sat down with her friends to eat a lunch of lasagne and salad.

'That Celia Reed's a pain!' she exclaimed.

'She's good at maths,' said Poppy.

'Oh, she's a creep,' said Cassie dismissively. 'And she's always following Abigail around everywhere, trying to suck up to her.'

To cheer herself up, Cassie suggested taking Mitsi and Poppy to see the folly after lunch, while Emily went to see Mr Green about starting flute lessons. Cassie led the two girls over the lawns, through the orchard, where trees were heavy with plums and apples, to the edge of the small wood, where the folly was situated. Mitsi was immediately entranced by the crumbling ruin and vowed to come back another day with her camera. Poppy was not so impressed and soon started looking about her; it was not long before she spotted the roof and chimney of Mrs Allingham's cottage through the trees.

'Whose is the little house over there?' she asked.

Cassie hesitated to tell her about Mrs Allingham, as their friendship was still supposed to be a secret shared only by herself, Becky and Emily. The old lady had been very good to the girls, and they, in turn, had made themselves useful to her. She had once taught at Redwood, and had since retired to the little cottage.

'Oh, just some old lady's cottage,' she replied carelessly. 'Come on, I'd like to get back now.'

As they turned their backs on the folly, Poppy put her hand on Cassie's shoulder.

'Did you hear something?'

'No,' answered Cassie. 'Did you, Mitsi?'

'No. What did you think you heard, Poppy?'

'I don't know. Just a funny little noise,' she said. 'Never mind. It must have been my imagination.'

When they rejoined Emily, she chattered on nineteen to the dozen about her first flute lesson. It was a great novelty to her, as she had not learned an instrument in the first year. By coincidence, the first lesson of the afternoon was music with Mr Green. As they filed into the music room, he took Cassie to one side.

'I've got some good news for you,' he said. 'The examination results came through this morning.'

'Oh, did I pass?' asked Cassie. She had taken her Grade Three Violin exam towards the end of the previous term.

'Not just a pass, young lady. A distinction!'

He gave her her mark-sheet and certificate and she looked at both with delight. When the class had all settled at their tables, Mr Green played them a tape of the *William Tell* overture. Towards the end of the lesson, he asked the new boys and girls if any of them already played an instrument. Poppy was already learning the cornet, which pleased Mr Green, as he had no trumpets in his orchestra so far. A couple of boys played the clarinet and another girl the piano. Mitsi asked if she could begin viola lessons and Mr Green readily agreed. Then Celia Reed put up her hand.

'Yes, Celia?' said Mr Green.

'Please sir,' she said smarmily, 'I have Grade Five Piano and Grade Four Flute.'

'Well, that's excellent, Celia. You'll be able to join the school orchestra straight away.'

'Typical,' Cassie thought to herself, but without envy. Nothing could shake her happiness just then.

The afternoon passed quickly and in no time at all Cassie was packing away her homework from her desk, looking forward to the character class, which was their last lesson before supper at six-thirty.

'I like these character skirts!' exclaimed Poppy, twirling around in her full black skirt, with its colourful ribbons.

'They are rather plain,' said Mitsi. 'Have you ever seen the traditional Japanese costumes?'

'No,' said Poppy. 'Are they nice?'

'They're *gorgeous*,' said Mitsi. 'I shall ask Mummy to send me one of ours in the post, to show you all.'

'Won't that cost a lot?' asked Cassie.

'No matter. She won't mind. I'll dance in it for you.'

'That would be great, Mitsi,' said Cassie, thinking that having a costume here at school might perhaps remind her of home.

'What's the character dance teacher like?' asked Poppy, still twirling her skirt.

'She's very nice,' Emily piped up. 'She's called Mrs Bonsing. She's short and rather fat, but ever so light on her feet. You'll like her, I'm sure.'

Despite her reservations about national dances other than Japanese, Mitsi excelled in the character class and Mrs Bonsing soon had her demonstrating a *Tarantella*, which most of the other students had found difficult to learn.

'Lovely, Mitsuko!' she exclaimed at the end of the demonstration. 'I can see you're a natural.'

Mitsi beamed with pleasure. It was the first time in the last three days that Cassie had seen her look really happy.

Later, at supper, Cassie and Emily found themselves alone at their table while Mitsi and Poppy were still in the queue. Cassie took the opportunity of asking Emily if she thought they should let Poppy and Mitsi in on the secret about Mrs Allingham.

'Well, *I* wouldn't mind,' said Emily. 'But the thing is, Becky's not here to ask, is she?'

'No. We'll have to leave it till next week and ask her then.'

'I'm sure she'll agree,' said Emily. 'I mean, it's not as though it's a *very* secret secret, is it?'

As she finished her sentence, Celia sat down at the table with her supper tray.

'Ooh, secrets,' she said. 'I like secrets.'

Cassie stuck her chin out firmly. 'It wouldn't be a secret if we told you.'

'Oh, go on,' Celia pleaded in a rather whingeing tone. 'Don't be a spoil-sport.'

Mitsi and Poppy joined their table. 'Who's being a spoil-sport?' laughed Poppy.

'Cassie,' complained Celia. 'She won't tell me the big secret.'

'It's not a big secret,' Cassie snapped, beginning to feel irritated.

'Well, then, you can tell us!' said Celia.

'No fear,' said Cassie. She noticed a hurt expression on Mitsi's face, but couldn't say anything to her in Celia's hearing. Luckily, Celia grew bored with pestering and went off to get her pudding.

'Oh, thank goodness for that!' sighed Emily.

Cassie turned to Mitsi and Poppy. 'We *have* got a secret that we want to share with you, but we need to wait till Becky comes back – OK?'

'Sounds mysterious,' said Poppy. 'But I can wait four or five days.'

Mitsi nodded her agreement, looking relieved. 'When can we go back to that folly again?' she asked. 'I want to take some pictures. I bet it would look beautiful in the moonlight.'

Cassie leaned forward across the table. 'Last year, we went across to it one night when it was dark, and had a midnight feast there. It was ace!'

'Where was this?' asked a voice at her elbow. Celia had returned with her pudding. Cassie quickly changed the subject, making a mental note to be on her guard in future, while there was any possibility of Celia being in earshot. As she seemed to be Mrs Ramsbottom's favourite, Celia was the last person to tell about breaking school rules.

With a sudden pang, Cassie remembered her detention. There would be little time for recreation tonight. Nevertheless, she promised herself a bath before bed, in which she could lie and dream about dancing as a little swan with the Birmingham Royal Ballet.

4

A White Mouse

Cassie felt excited all through the following Sunday, wondering what time Becky would arrive at school. In the end, it was quite late in the afternoon when Mr and Mrs Hastings brought her back. The three of them looked tanned and well: Becky had regained the fullness in her cheeks and the sparkle in her eyes.

'Oh, I'm so pleased to see you!' cried Cassie, giving her friend a big hug. She was quickly followed by Emily, and then they introduced Mitsi and Poppy to Becky, who had been surprised to see totally new faces in the bedroom.

'I'll help you unpack now, dear,' offered Becky's mother, beginning to unzip her suitcase.

'No, Mum, it's all right,' said Becky, holding the lid firmly down. 'I can do it myself.'

'But darling, you know you get so tired.'

'I'm fine, Mum, honestly. You go off now with Dad. I've got to get used to looking after myself again.'

Mrs Hastings sighed, but gave in. She had worried herself sick ever since Becky had been taken ill and found it hard to believe she was really better.

'Go on, Dad,' urged Becky. 'Tell her I'll be all right.'

'She *will* be all right, you know,' said Mr Hastings confidently. 'Cheerio, love. We'll see you soon.'

Mrs Hastings stooped down to kiss her daughter goodbye, for she was a tall woman. 'And just be *careful*, Rebecca. Don't go over-taxing your strength.'

'No, Mum.'

'I don't know, Ron,' she said, turning to her husband, 'do you think the specialist was right about Becky coming back?'

'Well, dear, he did say it was the best form of rehabilitation he could think of. All the exercise will help her to regain the suppleness of her back. It's still very stiff at the moment, isn't it, Becky?'

'Yes, Dad.'

'And your balance too,' added her mum. 'However will you cope with all the turning steps?'

'I'll cope,' said Becky firmly. She appealed to her dad with her eyes.

'Come on then, dear,' he said, taking the hint. 'Let's leave these young ladies to get on with it.'

Once goodbyes had been said, and the door closed

on her parents, Becky flung open the lid of her large suitcase and snatched out a small box.

'You seemed keen to get rid of your mum and dad,' Cassie commented, watching her actions curiously.

'Too true!' cried Becky. 'I thought they were never going to go.'

She opened the box carefully and lifted out the contents.

'Oh, a mouse!' shrieked Mitsi, going pale.

A tiny white mouse lay in the palm of Becky's hand. It had pink eyes and a pink nose. Becky stroked it tenderly.

'Meet Columbus,' she said.

Cassie laughed at the name. 'Is this one of Button and Cotton's babies?'

'No,' corrected Becky. 'This is one of their grandchildren.'

'Isn't he cute?' purred Poppy. 'May I hold him for a bit?'

'Sure,' said Becky. 'You hold him while I sort out a bite to eat.'

'For you or the mouse?' Cassie asked.

'The mouse, you twit,' said Becky.

Mitsi had withdrawn to the farthest wall. She still looked very white.

'Ouch!' yelled Poppy. 'He bit me!' She let the mouse go hurriedly and he ran over the beds and zigzagged across the carpet.

'Catch him!' Becky shouted. Mitsi bit back a squeal as the others scrambled round the room, giggling, in their efforts to recapture Columbus. He found himself cornered, ran headlong up Mitsi's back and dived down the neck of her shirt.

'Oiee!' she shrilled as Columbus wriggled down her sleeve. Becky, Cassie and Poppy were helpless with laughter. Only Emily understood Mitsi's terror, and was quietly retrieving the mouse from her shirt, when Mrs Ramsbottom strode in.

'What is the meaning of this?' she demanded.

Emily's hand had fortunately just closed on Columbus and so she quickly hid him behind her back, praying he wouldn't bite her. Cassie, Poppy and Becky sheepishly picked themselves up from the floor.

'Well?' she asked, glaring at Mitsuko, who was still rigid with fright. 'You look as if you've seen a ghost. What silly game have you been playing?'

'That's it,' said Cassie, grateful for her housemother's suggestion. 'We were telling each other ghost stories and Mitsi got scared.'

'Well, I'm sure there's no need to scream the place down,' said Mrs Ramsbottom sharply. 'Take a black mark, Mitsuko. Perhaps it'll remind you not to give vent to your feelings like that in future.'

'Yes, Mrs Ramsbottom,' whispered poor Mitsi, staring at the floor.

'Now, will the five of you get on with something sensible. Rebecca, I see you've arrived at last. Holidays in term-time are not *my* way at all, but I suppose Miss Wrench had a good reason for giving you a week's leave.'

She left the room as abruptly as she had entered it.

Becky gazed at the door in amazement. 'Who was that?' she managed to ask.

'Our new housemother,' answered Cassie glumly.

'But what's happened to Miss Eiseldown?'

'She's gone to America,' said Emily.

Becky shook her head in disbelief. 'Where's Columbus?' she asked, suddenly remembering the cause of all the rumpus.

'It's all right, Becky,' said Emily, holding out her hand. 'I've got him safe.'

'Oh, thank goodness,' said Becky. 'I kept expecting him to pop up when that awful woman was here. He's my favourite mouse. That's why I decided to bring him to school with me.'

She put Columbus back in his box with some food and placed it in the wardrobe. 'He can go to sleep when he's had his supper.'

'Are you OK now, Mitsi?' asked Emily.

'I don't like mice,' said Mitsi, still trembling a little. 'It was horrible when it went down my shirt. Ugh!'

'He wouldn't hurt you,' said Becky, who was unable to sympathise with Mitsi's fear.

'Oh I don't know,' said Poppy. 'He gave my thumb a good nip!'

Fortunately, over the next few days, Mitsi grew used to having tiny Columbus scurrying round the room after supper. It was too dangerous to let him out in the mornings, because Mrs Ramsbottom never knocked before coming in for room inspection.

'That woman is driving me mad,' said Becky after one of Mrs Ramsbottom's unwelcome visits. 'She manages to find specks of dirt the size of a microbe!'

'I know,' agreed Cassie. 'She put me in detention before you came back.'

Becky sighed. 'I sometimes wonder what I'm doing back here. It's not as though I'm keeping up with you all in ballet any more.'

Miss Wrench had been willing to take Becky back, on the doctor's recommendation, but had arranged for her to take her ballet classes with the first years, as she had lost so much ground.

'Never mind, Becky,' said Cassie. 'You'll soon catch up. And it's not as though you've fallen behind in any of your other subjects.'

'Oh, I've just remembered,' Poppy interrupted. 'Madame Larette's going to tell us more about the *Swan Lake* audition this evening. Sorry, Becky,' she added guiltily, 'I forgot you wouldn't be able to take part.'

'Oh, you needn't worry,' Becky replied. 'I've no desire whatever to be a swan on stage.'

In the lunch hour, as Mitsi and Poppy were both involved in instrumental lessons, Cassie, Becky and Emily found themselves alone for the first time since Becky's return.

'We've been wanting to ask you something,' said Cassie, as they strolled through the rose garden. 'Should we tell Mitsi and Poppy about Mrs Allingham?'

'I don't see why not,' answered Becky. 'If you're sure they'd keep it to themselves.'

'Yes, I think they would,' said Emily.

'OK, then, we'll tell them later,' said Cassie. 'How

about slipping across now to say hello?'

They crossed the massive lawns, wound through the orchard and past the folly, reaching the edge of the wood, where the old lady's cottage snuggled. The gardens were looking tidy and colourful with fuchsias and roses still in bloom. The hedge had been clipped and even the ivy on the walls cut back.

Mrs Allingham was delighted to see them. 'Oh, it seems so long since the summer term!' she exclaimed. 'My, Cassie, you've sprouted!'

Cassie nodded ruefully.

'And how are you now, Becky dear? I'm so glad you were able to come back to the ballet school.'

'Oh, I'm fine now, thank you, Mrs Allingham,' Becky replied. 'Your garden's looking very nice.'

'Do you think so? Well, thank you. I've been very fortunate in obtaining the services of a first-rate gardener. He's called Arthur, you know.'

'Would you like us to do a few jobs in the house?' asked Cassie.

'Well now, that *would* be kind. I do find the stairs very difficult to clean, with my back trouble, you know.'

After a spot of cleaning, the girls were rewarded as usual with some tasty home-made biscuits and a glass of fruit juice.

'Mmm, these are nice,' said Cassie. 'I can taste something spicy.'

'Yes, there's cinnamon in them,' said Mrs Allingham. 'Now, tell me the news from school.'

'There *is* some exciting news actually,' said Cassie.

'The Birmingham Royal Ballet company want some second and third years to audition for the "Dance of the Little Swans" '.

'That would be a wonderful experience,' said the old lady, rubbing her arthritic hands together. 'I remember when I was young, and I danced that part.'

'Did you, Mrs Allingham?' Emily asked.

'Yes. I wasn't much older than you. It was my first professional engagement. I'll never forget it. You don't, when it's your first, you know. I was with a lovely crowd of girls. All the same height we were. And our costumes were beautiful. Even now, I can feel the swansdown that we had in our head-dresses.'

'Did you have a white tutu?' asked Cassie.

'No. The little swans have calf-length net dresses, with satin bodices. And I remember we had to have special white satin ballet shoes. Not the usual pink!'

As Mrs Allingham reminisced, Cassie wondered if she would have similar memories one day. She did hope so – the idea of dancing with the Birmingham Royal Ballet was so wonderful.

On their way back past the folly, Cassie thought she heard a noise. 'Poppy thought she heard something the other day,' she said.

'It sounded like a kitten mewing to me,' said Becky, straining her ears. She hunted round the ruined building, until she heard the mewing. Then she was able to find what she was looking for, sheltering under an overhanging stone.

'Come and look,' she whispered. 'A mother cat – she must be a stray – and two kittens.'

'Oh aren't they adorable!' said Emily.

Cassie reached out to pick one of them up.

'No, leave them,' said Becky. 'We'll frighten the mother into moving them if we disturb them. Then we might never find them again.'

The girls stooped down, quietly gazing at the animals. The kittens were quite unlike one another. One was stripy and ginger, like its mother. The other was black with a white nose and bib and four white paws.

'Doesn't their mother look thin?' Cassie hissed.

'Yes, she's half-starved,' agreed Becky. 'We must bring her some food tonight. She's got to feed these two as well as herself.'

'Just make sure you don't bring Columbus with you!' Cassie joked.

They heard the bell for afternoon lessons clanging in the distance, and tore themselves away from the kittens.

'Thank goodness it isn't maths,' puffed Cassie, as they sprinted back over the lawns.

She found afternoon school quite boring – her mind wouldn't stay on her work for more than a few minutes together. At last came the meeting with Madame, when she was to tell them more about *Swan Lake*.

'The auditions are to be 'eld three weeks from today,' Madame announced. 'At two-thirty in the afternoon. A minibus will collect you at one-thirty from school, so you will 'ave plenty of time to change.'

When excited mutters broke out in the class,

Madame clapped her hands together. '*Maintenant, mes élèves*, we must get down to the work, *n'est-ce pas?*'

Cassie was delighted to find that, instead of pointe-work practice which they were expecting, Madame was going to teach them part of the 'Dance of the Little Swans'. They worked separately while they learned the basic sequence of steps, but Madame promised that next time they would be able to dance in groups, just like the real thing.

Mitsi and Poppy seemed to have found some new friends to sit with at supper-time, so Cassie, Becky and Emily made room on their table for Matthew and Tom.

'You look like the cat that got the cream,' Matthew remarked to Cassie.

'Oh, do I?' asked Cassie. 'Well, I haven't got it yet. Just hoping!'

Emily explained to the boys about the *Swan Lake* auditions.

'Don't they want any boy cygnets?' Matthew asked, mock-wistfully.

Cassie laughed. 'It was funny you should mention cats,' she said.

'I thought I said "cygnets".'

'No, silly, when you first sat down.'

'Oh, yes?'

'Well, we found some today,' Cassie went on. 'At the folly. Two kittens and a mother cat.'

'That reminds me,' said Becky. 'Save a bit of your fish, everyone.'

'I'm too hungry,' said Matthew, about to put the last piece of his into his mouth.

Cassie knocked it off his fork and snatched it off the table. 'The cats need it more than you!' she cried.

'Aren't you even allowed to eat your own food around here?' Matthew complained, good-humouredly.

'Guess what!' said Cassie, laughing. 'Becky's brought a mouse to school with her.'

'Oh, I like mice!' said Tom.

'Mitsi doesn't!' said Emily. 'It scared her to death the first day when it ran down her shirt.'

'Can we come and see it?' asked Matthew. 'What's it called, anyway?'

'Columbus,' said Becky. 'You could come up tomorrow lunch-time, if you like.'

Having fixed a time for mouse-viewing, the girls went off to find Poppy and Mitsi. They had already told them about the cats and had arranged an expedition to the folly that evening.

Cassie had crammed several scraps of fish, rolled in a paper napkin, into her track suit pocket. She had caught a glimpse of Celia Reed looking over at their table, so she headed across the dining-hall, in the opposite direction, flanked by Becky and Emily.

Unfortunately, she hadn't reckoned with having to pass close by Mrs Ramsbottom, who was on dinner duty. The housemother looked suspiciously at Cassie and stopped her.

'Take your hands out of your pockets, girl,' she barked.

'Yes, Mrs Ramsbottom,' answered Cassie, removing her hand and just hoping that the fishy bundle wouldn't become visible.

Luckily it wasn't spotted, and Cassandra and her friends quickly left the hall.

When they had joined Poppy and Mitsi, Cassie suggested going to the folly straight away, while they knew Mrs Ramsbottom was still in the dining-hall, and while it was still light. After Mitsi had collected her camera, they let themselves out of the back entrance to their wing and made their way cautiously across the lawns.

'I just hope Celia isn't anywhere about!' Cassie remarked. 'She'll be sure to spot us if she is.'

When they reached the folly, all was silent. Becky went straight to the cats' 'nest', but it was deserted. She stood up, disappointed.

'What a shame!'

The others gathered round.

'Oh, I wanted to see the kittens,' complained Poppy.

'I think I'll take one or two photos anyway,' said Mitsi, taking the lens cover off her camera.

After photographing the folly, she caught up with the others and they made their way rather dejectedly back to school. In the twilight, mist clung to the contours of the lawn. The large school building looked at that moment more like some romantic moorland manorhouse.

'We'll have to come back in the daytime and search for them,' said Cassie, gazing ahead. Through the mist, she could make out the outline of someone standing

44

in the doorway of the back entrance.

'Stop, all of you,' she whispered. 'There's someone at the door. Follow me; we'll go round the side to the fire-escape.'

'It'll be locked,' said Emily.

'Oh blast, I'd forgotten. Well at least we can hide there for a while.'

Mitsi shivered. 'It feels damp out here.'

As Cassie hesitated, the figure at the door came forwards towards them, beckoning with one arm.

'I wonder who it is?' said Becky.

The girls thought they had better start walking towards the figure, which now stood still, its face in shadow, its arms folded.

'It looks a bit like . . .'

'Oh, no!' said Cassie.

A few steps closer, and there was no doubt in anyone's mind that the figure was Mrs Ramsbottom.

'Now we're for it!' whispered Cassie.

5

Mouse on the Loose

The girls were still smarting from their confrontation with Mrs Ramsbottom the night before as they made their beds and tidied and cleaned their room the following morning. When the housemother arrived, she hardly glanced at the room or the beds. She was more concerned with giving them another lecture (they had already had one the previous night) about breaking school rules.

'You know *quite* well that you are not allowed into the grounds after supper. And yet you deliberately defied that rule. You will all remain in detention this evening.'

The girls didn't dare groan until Mrs Ramsbottom

was well down the corridor. They had just started complaining about their punishment, when there was a knock on the door and Lesley, their first year neighbour, put her head round it.

'Did you get done last night?' she asked.

'Shh!' said Mitsi. 'Mrs Ramsbottom might hear you.'

'It's all right. I watched her go.'

'Yes,' said Cassie, in reply to Lesley's question. 'She was waiting for us when we came back. How did you know about it?'

'I overheard Celia telling Mrs Ramsbottom that she had seen you all going out into the grounds.'

'I knew it!' cried Cassie. 'I knew Celia would be at the bottom of it!'

'That girl needs a good shake,' said Poppy angrily.

'Hadn't we better be going down to ballet class?' said Mitsi timidly.

'Oh, yes!' cried Cassie. 'Look at the time!'

Cassie felt pleased to be able to forget all about Mrs Ramsbottom and her petty rules and regulations, when she was dancing. It was strange, really, she thought to herself, how ballet enforced a very strict discipline on you too, but one which you didn't mind, because you loved what it taught you. To feel absolutely in control of his or her body was what a dancer aimed for; there were moments already when Cassie could feel she was getting near that supreme aim.

But it was a constant struggle; there were so many things that had to be practised over and over again and so many steps which she wished she could

48

perform better. She was ever conscious of the other girls in the class – her competitors as well as her friends – especially Abigail, Poppy and Emily. Abigail had quickly taken the position, vacated by Amanda, of Miss Oakland's favourite student, and Cassie envied her ease of movement and great self-assurance.

On their way to the next lesson, after an indoor break due to wet weather, Cassie touched on how she felt to Becky.

'But Abi's really nice,' said Becky in surprise. 'Not a bit like Amanda.'

'That's not what I'm saying,' said Cassie. 'It just makes me uneasy, that's all, because I think she's a better dancer than I am.'

'You can't always be best,' said Becky.

Cassie felt a little hurt that Becky didn't understand, but resolutely pushed it to the back of her mind as they entered the science lab. Their science teacher, Mr Adderley, had marked the assignments on energy, which they'd handed in the week before, and was waiting to hand them out. He was an old-fashioned, very formal teacher, and always gave out homework and exam papers in order of merit, starting with the highest mark.

How awful to be the bottom of the heap, thought Cassie. She always managed to be somewhere in the middle in science, while Becky was always top. Becky had a flair for maths and science and was secretly hoping to qualify as a vet.

Mr Adderley held up the assignment at the top of his pile. It looked amazingly thick. Becky must have done loads of work, thought Cassie.

'An excellent piece of work. Thoroughly researched,' he said. But instead of calling out 'Rebecca Hastings' as usual, he called 'Celia Reed'.

Cassie looked at Becky. Her friend had gone even whiter than normal.

'Celia must have put hours in to do an assignment that long,' whispered Cassie.

'She's a swot,' said Becky indignantly.

Cassie couldn't help smiling to herself. Now Becky had tasted some of what she had been feeling about Abigail!

It was still wet at lunch-time and the girls were glad of Columbus to keep them entertained in their room. Becky was just feeding him some cornflakes saved from breakfast when Celia came in, without knocking. Becky popped Columbus into her pocket in a reflex action and was pretty sure that Celia hadn't seen him.

'Do you *have* to come barging into our room without knocking?' Cassie complained, frowning.

'You've got nothing to hide, have you?' asked Celia coldly.

'No, but we've seen that you're pretty good at poking your nose into other people's business,' Cassie retorted.

Celia laughed. 'Got the wrong person there.'

'No, I don't think we have,' said Cassie.

'Nor me,' said Poppy. 'I know what I'd like to do with you, you little sneak.'

Celia backed towards the door. She didn't like the look in Poppy's green eyes.

'See you later, alligators,' she called, ducking out of the door. Not long after, when Matthew and Tom arrived to meet Columbus, Cassie told them about their disastrous visit to the folly, and Celia's part in it all.

'We'd better not stay long then,' said Matthew. 'Don't want to get you into any more trouble. Ouch! This mouse of yours nips, doesn't he?'

'He never bites me,' said Becky, a trifle huffily.

'Well, yours is the hand that feeds him, I suppose,' said Tom.

'Why don't we go and have a look for the kittens now?' suggested Cassie, looking out of the window. 'The rain's stopped.'

'Count me out,' said Matthew. 'I don't like getting my feet wet.'

'Nor me,' said Tom.

The girls were all glad to get out for a breath of fresh air.

'Ooh, it's good to put a bit of space between us and Celia,' said Poppy. 'She's really getting to me.'

As they tramped over the wet lawn, Emily wondered if this was such a good idea. Their shoes would have to be cleaned really well before they could take them back into their room.

They found the kittens quite easily this time. Their mother had brought them back to the folly, half-way up the tower. Once Becky had enticed the mother down with the fish scraps they'd brought, the children were able to handle the kittens.

'Oh, isn't he lovely!' cooed Becky, holding the black

and white one. 'He's my favourite.'

'We ought to give them names,' said Cassie. 'How about Mop and Bucket?'

The others laughed. 'Or Punch and Judy?' suggested Emily.

'No,' said Becky. 'This one's Tinker – it suits him perfectly.

'And what about the other one?' asked Poppy. 'You choose, Cassie.'

'How about Marmalade?'

'Purrrr-fect,' said Poppy. 'Don't you want to hold him, Mitsi?'

'No thank you,' said Mitsi stiffly. She was standing on the lowest step of the tower. 'I don't like animals.'

'I don't know how you can say that,' said Becky, stroking little Tinker's head. 'Look at him – he's licking my cardigan. He must think I'm his mother!'

'Ah, isn't he sweet,' said Cassie. 'Hand him over, now, Becky. I haven't had a turn yet.'

But soon the mother cat had finished her scraps and, reluctantly, the children had to leave the kittens to her care. There was just time for them to return to their room, to pick up the school-books they would need for the afternoon.

'Hang on,' said Becky. 'I'll just check Columbus is OK before I go.' She opened his box in the wardrobe and gave a little shriek.

'He's gone! Columbus has gone!'

'He must be in the wardrobe then,' said Cassie. 'Let me look!'

But Columbus was not in the wardrobe either. Becky started searching the room frantically.

'Come on, Becky,' said Cassie. 'You'll be late for French. As long as we close the door behind us, he won't get far, will he?'

'I'm sure we'll find him later,' said Emily, pulling Becky's arm.

Becky looked worried for the rest of the afternoon, and Cassie guessed that she was dying to get back to the bedroom.

The first opportunity came in homework period. Becky, naturally, was first back at the room.

'I just can't understand how he got out of the wardrobe!' she said, as Cassie came in with the others.

'It is strange,' said Cassie. 'But he's got to be here somewhere.'

The girls searched the room thoroughly but there was no sign of Columbus anywhere.

'I'll go and ask down the landing,' said Emily.

'I'll come with you,' offered Poppy.

A few minutes later they returned, but without any news of Columbus.

'Oh dear,' said Becky. 'I feel really worried about him.'

Cassie sat down on her bed. 'He can't really have got out on his own, can he?'

'No,' said Becky glumly.

'Then that means someone has let him out deliberately.'

'Or taken him to keep as their own pet,' added Poppy.

'It wasn't you, was it, Mitsi?' Becky said suddenly, turning on the Japanese girl.

'No of course not! I don't like mice!'

'Oh I didn't mean to keep. I meant you might have helped him to run away because you didn't like him in the room.'

Tears sprang into Mitsi's eyes. 'How can you think I would do such a thing?' she cried.

'Oh I'm sorry,' said Becky, as suddenly apologetic as she had been accusing. 'I'm not thinking straight. But *who has* taken Columbus?'

'It may have been the boys,' said Cassie slowly. 'You know what they're like for practical jokes.'

Becky brightened up at this suggestion and actually managed to get down to some geography homework.

As soon as the girls arrived in the studio for character class, their last lesson of the day, Becky rushed over to Matthew.

'Come on, where is he?' she demanded.

'Who?' asked a surprised Matthew.

'Columbus, of course. What have you done with him?'

'Excuse *me*,' interrupted Mrs Bonsing. 'This is a dance lesson, not a time for gossip. Now boys, let's see you do the Hornpipe, shall we?'

Becky could hardly contain her impatience, but she had no further opportunity to speak to Matthew and Tom during the lesson. Mrs Bonsing asked Mitsi if she would show the class one of the traditional Japanese dances that her father had taught her.

This came as something of a surprise to the friends.

Their shy little Mitsi was transformed as soon as she started the dance; she glowed with a confidence they had never seen in her before.

Everyone applauded her when she'd finished.

'That was wonderful, Mitsuko,' said Mrs Bonsing. 'Thank you so much for showing us your dance.' She made a Japanese-style bow to her pupil, to which Mitsi responded solemnly.

On their way out of the studio, Cassie caught up with Mitsi.

'Is your father a dancer, then, Mitsi?' she asked.

'Yes,' replied Mitsi. 'A professional dancer in the traditional Japanese theatre. The dances are passed on from father to son.'

'But you're a girl!' Cassie exclaimed.

Mitsi smiled shyly. 'My father has no sons, and I begged him to teach me, so he did.'

Meanwhile, Becky was interrogating Matthew.

'Well?' she demanded, hands on hips.

'I haven't got him,' said Matthew. 'Last time I saw him was when we were all together in your room. Honest!'

Becky's face fell and even when she returned to the bedroom after supper it was still a mile long.

'Oh come on, cheer up, Becky,' said Cassie. 'I can't stand it when you're miserable. Someone's bound to come across Columbus soon!'

As she finished speaking, they heard terrible shrieks from the floor above. They looked at one another. Becky was wide-eyed.

'That's Mrs Ramsbottom's room above us,' she said.

'You don't think she's found . . . ?'

Cassie didn't have time to finish her question as Becky was already heading for the door. The girls rushed upstairs. When they reached Mrs Ramsbottom's door, they found it open. The shrieks, as loud as ever, were unmistakably issuing from the housemother's room.

Cassie steeled herself to look in. When she did, a very comical sight met her eyes. Mrs Ramsbottom was perched precariously upon her small desk, while the tiny white mouse scampered nervously about her carpet.

'Take that rodent out of here!' yelled Mrs Ramsbottom, as soon as she noticed the girls. 'Whose is it?'

'Mine, Mrs Ramsbottom,' said Becky, immediately catching Columbus and taking him back to his box.

Cassie was about to follow her when Mrs Ramsbottom stopped her. She looked very angry.

'Tell Rebecca to take another detention,' she snapped. 'And also tell her to take her rodent to Miss Wrench's office. I'll inform her immediately that it's to be confiscated.'

She strode off in the direction of the office, while Cassie reluctantly went off to tell Becky the bad news.

6

Night Noises

The outcome of her interview with Miss Wrench was that although Becky could not be allowed to keep Columbus at school, at least he would come to no harm. A phone call to Becky's father ensured that the mouse would have a free ride back home the next day.

Although she was terribly relieved about Columbus's fate, Becky was still furious with Mrs Ramsbottom.

'I mean,' she said the following morning, 'she was talking about confiscating him, as though he were a bag of sweets or something.'

'I think she was very cross that we had found her screaming at him,' said Cassie.

'I'd love to know who let him out,' said Becky. 'Whoever it was probably planted him in Mrs Ramsbottom's room deliberately.'

'Perhaps Celia did spot him that time she barged into our room.'

'Yes, perhaps she did,' said Becky. 'Well, in that case – war on Celia! And war on Mrs Ramsbottom!'

'Well, you can't be sure about Celia,' said Emily.

'I don't know who else would have done it,' argued Cassie. 'Anyway, I agree with Becky about Mrs Ramsbottom. She's made life hard for us. Let's make life hard for her.'

'We'll have to cook up some ideas,' said Becky, her eyes sparkling with pleasure at what lay in store for their unpopular housemother.

During the rest of the week, the girls continued to visit the cat family every lunch-hour, feeding the mother cat with scraps saved from the night before. The kittens were growing fast and becoming more playful. It was lovely to watch them romping with one another and jumping on each other's backs. Their mother was beginning to lose her starved appearance and had grown to trust the girls with her offspring. Becky always made a great fuss of her favourite, Tinker, and the others had little chance to hold him when she came with them.

At the same time, they were hatching plans against Mrs Ramsbottom, putting the first one into action that very weekend. Recently they had noticed an enormous, large-bodied black spider creeping around their bathroom. Mitsi was terrified of it and more than once implored Becky to put it out of the window. But Becky thought this was cruel, and refused. No one else dared touch it.

Then Cassie came up with a plan which would both rid their bathroom of the pest and, with luck, disturb Mrs Ramsbottom's peace.

'If she's afraid of mice, you can bet she's afraid of spiders,' she pointed out.

'Just like me,' said Mitsi ruefully.

'Whereabouts in her room do you want me to put it?' asked Becky, rubbing her hands together gleefully.

'Her bath?' suggested Emily.

'Her bed?' proposed Cassie.

'No, I've got it,' said Poppy. 'Her underwear drawer. He won't be able to escape from there!'

'Oh, poor spider!' said Becky, with such consternation that everyone fell about laughing.

The event was planned for Saturday afternoon, when they knew Mrs Ramsbottom would be safely out of the way, taking students into the village to spend their pocket-money.

The morning turned out fine, which was a good omen, as the afternoon walk would have been cancelled had it been raining.

Ballet class was taken by Madame Larette, as she wanted to carry on teaching the girls their audition parts for the 'Dance of the Little Swans'. As she had promised, she put them into groups, four or five in each, and showed them how to link hands behind their backs in the traditional manner. The steps of the dance *felt* better done in a group, at least when everyone kept together, which wasn't often. Cassie began to realise how much practice they were going to need before the audition, to have any chance of success.

After class, the girls went back to the bedroom to change.

'Now we'd better decide who's going to stay and do the deed,' said Cassie. 'If none of us go into the village, it's going to look mighty suspicious!'

'I don't want to stay,' said Mitsi with a shudder. 'Just thinking about that spider makes my hair stand on end.'

'OK,' said Cassie. 'What about you, Emily?'

'I think I'll go with Mitsi,' she replied.

'That leaves three of us. D'you think that's OK?' Cassie asked.

'Sounds fine,' said Becky. 'We'll need at least one of us to stand guard.'

'What about Celia?' asked Poppy.

'Let's hope she goes on the walk.'

'But what if she doesn't?'

'We'd better find out at lunch,' said Cassie. 'If she's staying around, we'll have to keep her well out of the way.'

'Yes, we know what a tittle-tattle she is,' said Becky.

In the dining-hall, it was Emily's job to stand 'accidentally' near Celia in the dinner queue and make conversation with her, to find out her plans for the afternoon.

'We've got problems,' said Emily as she joined the others with her tray of lemon chicken and rice. 'Celia's staying on the landing this afternoon. She says she's broke.'

'Oh no,' they all groaned in unison.

'I've got an idea,' said Cassie, 'which will keep her out of our hair, I think. Can you see Matthew and Tom anywhere?'

'Yes, they're over there, look!' pointed out Emily, who always noticed where everyone sat.

Cassie went over to sit with them when she had fetched her pudding, and asked for their help in keeping Celia off the landing.

'Leave it to us,' said Matthew. 'No problem. But why d'you want her out of the way?'

Cassie put her finger to her nose. 'Tell you later,' she said mysteriously.

All that was necessary now was to wait for Mrs Ramsbottom to leave the premises with her crocodile of girls. It was Poppy who gave the all clear before taking up her position as look-out on the landing. Bringing an empty sweet-box with her, Becky strode to the bathroom, accompanied by a more squeamish Cassie.

'Oh, I don't know how you can pick it up!' she squealed, as Becky swept up the spider and popped it in the box. 'It's such a big one!'

'Well, look at it from the spider's point of view. We're giants in relation to him.'

The girls passed Poppy on Mrs Ramsbottom's corridor, giving her a wink as they went by. Poppy glanced down the stairs and nodded to them as they paused outside Mrs Ramsbottom's door. There was no sign of life on the landing. Cassie and Becky opened the door and went in. Even though she knew full well that Mrs Ramsbottom was out, Cassie still half-expected her to spring out of her armchair and confront them.

'Come on,' said Becky. 'Don't look so nervous.'

They found a chest of drawers which housed some of Mrs Ramsbottom's clothing and tipped the spider into the top drawer.

'Hope she needs to go in there tomorrow,' said Becky.

A tap on the door made their blood freeze, but they relaxed when Poppy appeared.

'Hurry up, you two. It seems to be taking for ever.'

The girls scurried back to their bedroom, a little frustrated that now all they could do was wait. Emily and Mitsi wanted to hear all about it, of course, when they came back.

'We'll have to listen very carefully tomorrow morning from about half-past six when she's getting dressed,' said Emily.

'I'll set my watch alarm,' said Poppy. 'It'll be a pleasure for once to get up early.' The smile froze on her lips as she saw Celia Reed walk in.

'What d'you want to get up early for?' she asked in her usual nosey fashion.

'I don't know how you have the cheek to come in here!' exclaimed Poppy, her face almost as red as her hair. 'After what you did with Columbus.'

'Columbus? Who's Columbus?' asked Celia, all innocence.

'My mouse!' declared Becky.

'I don't know *what* you're talking about,' said Celia smugly. 'Hey, guess where I've been this afternoon?'

'Where have you been this afternoon?' echoed Cassie, a smile flitting across her lips.

'Down at the orchard. I had this mysterious letter, signed "Your Secret Admirer", asking me to meet him there at two o'clock.'

'And did he come?' asked Cassie.

'No, but I found *another* letter there. It was ever so exciting. You know, like in the films.'

Cassie tried hard to keep a straight face. 'And what did that letter say?'

'It said he was sorry he would probably be late, but to hang on for him until three o'clock, and if he couldn't get away then either, he would be in touch at a later date.'

'How romantic!' said Mitsi, who hadn't cottoned on to the trick Matthew and Tom had been playing on Celia. 'And did he come later?'

'No,' said Celia with a sigh. 'But when I was coming back across the lawns, I could see a boy waving from the boys' block. It was too far away to see who it was though.'

'Well, tell us if you get any more letters,' said Cassie, bursting to giggle. 'We'd better get down to supper now.'

It was a relief to laugh freely at their table in the dining-hall, with Celia out of earshot. Cassie thanked Matthew and Tom for their assistance and told them what they'd been up to while Celia was waiting for her 'secret admirer' in the orchard.

The next day, Sunday, Cassie, Becky and their friends woke when the watch alarm went off at six-thirty.

'I should think we've beaten Mrs Ramsbottom to it,' said Cassie. They dressed quietly, ears straining for sounds above them. But they had to wait nearly half an hour before they heard the housemother getting out of bed and padding about her room.

'I'm sure she's gone over to the chest of drawers,' whispered Cassie.

There was the faint sound of a drawer being pulled open and then a pause. The girls waited expectantly. Mrs Ramsbottom must be getting dressed now. Then at last came the sound they had been waiting for – a squeal of fear!

Amid muffled giggles, the girls shook hands with one another and Cassie and Becky were congratulated for having successfully accomplished their mission.

For once, they all had time on their hands. Everyone but Becky had a *Swan Lake* practice in the afternoon, but the whole morning was free, as they hadn't been set as much homework as usual. They decided to spend some extra time with the kittens, since it was a fine day. Taking the scraps saved from supper the night before, they walked across to the folly, enjoying the warm September sunshine.

'Oh look!' said Becky. 'There's a kestrel hovering

over there. He's probably seen a mouse.'

'Well, at least it's not Columbus, at any rate,' said Cassie. 'Are you missing him much, Becky?'

'No, not now I've got Tinker to play with.'

As they grew near to the folly, the little black kitten was the first to greet them. He trotted straight over to Becky and Becky gathered him up in her arms. The kittens would eat the odd scrap themselves now, even though they were still taking milk from their mother. Tinker stretched up on his hind legs to eat from Becky's hand, whereas Marmalade liked to eat with his four paws firmly on the ground. After the mother cat had devoured the remaining food greedily, she stretched out on the grass and began washing her legs.

'She really trusts us now,' said Becky. 'And when you think she was half-wild.'

The kittens started playing with one another, chasing each other's tails and rolling over and over together. When they'd tired of that, Tinker started rubbing his head against Becky's ankles, asking for another cuddle. But instead, Cassie teased him with a long piece of dried grass, dragging it along in front of him, to make him chase it. Tinker pounced on it a couple of times and then, disappointed it wasn't a real mouse's tail, stalked off to Becky once more.

Marmalade had allowed Emily to pick him up, but he wouldn't stay still for a minute. He climbed up her cardigan, across her shoulders, and even on top of her head. 'This one's a wriggle-bottom,' she said, laughing. Mitsi laughed too, but she wouldn't take

Marmalade when Poppy offered him to her. Cassie was amazed how Tinker snuggled up in Becky's arms, perfectly content.

'You've certainly got a way with animals, Becky,' she said, scratching the top of the kitten's head with one finger.

Their rehearsal in the afternoon went quite well, although Cassie found that some of her group weren't dancing quite in time with the music, which made the group effect a bit of a shambles. Becky had decided to go back to the folly after lunch to play with Tinker, as she had nothing else to keep her in school.

They all met again at supper-time, ravenous after the long rehearsal. Becky hadn't that excuse; she was just ravenous by nature. The fresh air and exercise, added to their early start, made them also very tired, and, when half-past eight came, there was no quiet chatting in the dormitory, just heads down on pillows, ready for a good night's sleep.

How long she'd been asleep she wasn't sure, but Cassie was suddenly awake again. What had woken her?

An unearthly wail reached her ears, making her shiver from the crown of her head to the tips of her toes.

'What was that?' whispered a terrified Mitsi, also by now awake.

'I don't know,' Cassie whispered back.

As the wailing began again, Cassie put on the light

and shook Poppy and Becky awake. Emily was already sitting up.

'Sounds really weird,' she said with shudder.

'Hush, let's listen!' hissed Becky.

'It sounds like a baby crying!' said Poppy.

The wailing stopped, but now they could hear some scrabbling noises outside, quickly followed by an unmistakable scratching at their window.

'Whatever is it?' said Mitsi, wide-eyed.

Becky and Cassie were already at the window, pulling back the curtains, to reveal a dark silhouette. Mitsi put the duvet over her head. A little white paw was scratching at the window-catch.

'It's Tinker!' whispered Becky in surprise. 'He must have climbed up the ivy on to the sill.'

The wailing had changed into his more familiar mewing now, as Cassie opened the window and let in the kitten.

Becky picked him up and stroked the white bib under his chin. 'I wonder if his mum knows he's out!'

'Oh, listen to him. He purrs like a lawn-mower!' said Cassie.

'Shall we give him some of the bits of meat from supper?' asked Emily.

After a few nibbles, Tinker became very playful and was soon tearing round the room, playing with crumpled pieces of paper out of the waste-paper basket. Then he found Emily's shoes and chewed the laces. After that, he started climbing on all the furniture, generally having a good nose round. Suddenly he flicked up his tail and charged up the curtains. Everybody burst out laughing as he clung there, staring at them with his wide eyes.

In their delight and excitement, the girls quite forgot Mrs Ramsbottom. She burst into the room just as Tinker was leaping from the curtains on to Cassie's bed.

'What is that . . . that animal doing in here?' she demanded. 'I suppose this is yet another of *your* pets, Rebecca Hastings!'

'No, Mrs Ramsbottom,' said Becky.

Cassie couldn't help smiling to herself at the image of trying to smuggle Tinker anywhere in a suitcase.

'Take that smile off your face, Cassandra Brown! Perhaps *you* will tell me whose this cat is?'

'It's no one's, Mrs Ramsbottom.'

'No one's? Of course it's someone's. Rebecca, I ask you again, is it one of your pets?'

'It *is* no one's,' Cassie persisted. 'There's a mother cat who shelters at the folly and this is one of her kittens.'

'I suppose you've been feeding them,' said Mrs Ramsbottom. 'Bringing them into school is quite stupid. Where are the others?' she asked, looking round the room.

'Oh, we didn't bring the kitten here,' said Cassie. 'The others are still outside. This one climbed up on to our window-sill and we opened the window when we found him there.'

'A likely tale,' snorted Mrs Ramsbottom. 'You're all in detention. And if you think you can pull the wool over my eyes, you're sadly mistaken.' She shook her head vehemently.

'Rebecca, you have permission to go down to the back entrance and put this animal outside, where he belongs. Now get into bed, the rest of you, and let's have no more disturbances.'

As Becky moved towards the door with Tinker, Mrs Ramsbottom had another thought. 'And I'll ask the caretaker in the morning to round up these scavenging cats and have them . . . *dealt with*.'

7

Tinker in Hiding

Before breakfast the next morning, Becky, Cassie, Emily and Poppy went over to the folly.

'We must get to them before the caretaker,' said Cassie. The idea of their beautiful kittens being taken away to a vet's to be put down had horrified all the girls.

There was no problem finding the cat family. As soon as the girls approached, Tinker and Marmalade came running out to greet them. After quickly giving them some food, Cassie picked up the little ginger one and Becky took up Tinker. Neither Poppy nor Emily could catch hold of the mother cat, however.

'Leave her,' said Becky. 'She's half-wild. She knows

how to hide and how to look after herself. I don't think for a moment the caretaker will be able to catch her.'

'D'you think it's all right to take them away from their mum?' asked Emily anxiously.

'They must be nearly weaned now,' answered Becky. 'They can eat solid food. And anyway, we haven't much choice, have we?'

'Come on then,' said Cassie decisively, cuddling Marmalade firmly to her chest. 'Let's get out of here quick.'

Once back in their room, the impossibility of keeping the kittens hidden dawned on them fully.

'Mrs Ramsbottom will be here in another quarter of an hour,' said Emily.

'Look, it would be much easier with *one* kitten,' said Cassie, watching the two little cats play-fighting. 'Quieter too!'

Tinker had nipped the tip of Marmalade's tail, causing Marmalade to yelp.

'I just hope Mrs Ramsbottom didn't hear that!' said Mitsi nervously.

'What are you getting at, Cassie?' asked Poppy.

'We can't save one and not the other!' said Becky indignantly.

'No, of course not,' said Cassie. 'That's not what I meant at all. I think we should take one of them to the boys' block. You know, spread the evidence about at bit.'

'Well, as long as it's Marmalade who goes,' said Becky, stroking her beloved Tinker.

'Right, then,' said Cassie. 'I'll take little Marmers over to Matthew and Tom straight away.'

'But someone might see you,' said Emily.

'I'll be careful. And it's still pretty early. Can you tidy up for me?'

'Sure,' said Becky. 'And I'll have a word with the first years across the way. They can hide Tink while Mrs Ramsbottom does her inspection, and then we can have him back when she does theirs.'

'Great,' said Cassie, opening the door and peeping out. 'All clear at the moment.' She slipped out, with Marmalade concealed under her blazer.

When, a few minutes later, she knocked on Matthew and Tom's door, their room-mate Ojo opened it and looked at her in surprise.

'Can I come in?' Cassie whispered urgently.

'Oh – yes . . .'

'What on earth are you doing here?' asked Matthew.

'Look,' said Cassie, producing the kitten from her blazer rather like a magician producing a rabbit from a hat. Ojo burst out laughing.

'What are you, some kind of magician?' he cried.

'Shut up, Ojo,' said Cassie. 'This is serious!' She turned to Matthew and Tom. 'Can you hide Marmalade for us? The caretaker's going to get rid of the kittens if he finds them, on Mrs Ramsbottom's orders.'

'Oh, that's horrible!' said Tom. 'Of course we'll hide him.'

'Oh, thanks,' said Cassie, with a sigh of relief. 'I knew I could count on you two.'

When she got back to her own room, Cassie was amazed to find all was orderly, clean and quiet.

'Where's Tinker?' she asked.

'I've taken him to Lesley's,' said Becky. ''Cause Mrs Ramsbottom comes here first. Did the boys agree to look after Marmalade?'

'No problem,' said Cassie.

Almost as if she sensed the thoughts of resentment and dislike that were coming from the girls in Room Twelve, Mrs Ramsbottom made her quickest inspection ever. As soon as she had left for the next room, Becky took up her empty school-bag – hers was the largest – and scurried over to Lesley's room, where she popped Tinker in it and scurried back.

'Now, behave yourself, Tinker,' she warned him, as she lifted him out again. 'You're to be quiet and good while Mrs Ramsbottom's on the landing.'

Indeed, the little black and white kitten behaved himself admirably for the next five minutes. The girls just hoped he wouldn't get up to any mischief while they were at breakfast and lessons.

Cassie couldn't really settle down properly to her exercises in ballet class, and she imagined Becky must be feeling just the same, in her first year class. She kept thinking of Tinker all alone in their room and wondering what he was getting up to. Unfortunately Miss Oakland, always sharp-eyed, saw that her concentration was wandering.

'Cassandra,' she said, stopping the pianist. 'Do I need to remind you this work is in preparation for your first major examination? If you don't pay

74

attention, how can you expect to learn?'

'Sorry, Miss Oakland.'

'You will be, Cassandra, when you fail your exam.' She sighed. 'Talent is not enough, you should know that by now. All the girls who come to Redwood have great potential – that's why they're chosen. Some fall by the wayside through ill health; a lot more because their bodies turn out to be the wrong shape or height. But of those that are left, what d'you think marks out the few who are going to succeed?'

'Genius, Miss Oakland?' Cassie ventured.

'Genius! Pff!' said Miss Oakland in a derogatory manner. 'It's not often any of us comes up against *genius*, Cassandra. No, dedication and sheer hard work, every time.' She laughed, which was unusual for her, and shook her head. 'Genius, indeed.'

At break, the girls rushed back to Room Twelve, only to find Becky had beaten them to it.

'I might have guessed you'd already be here,' said Cassie. Becky had saved some of her milk for the kitten and he was lapping it hungrily.

'Look, he's learned how to lap,' said Becky excitedly. 'So he must have been old enough to leave his mother.'

'It's getting a bit smelly in here,' said Mitsi.

'I'll have to empty his litter tray,' said Becky.

'Where did you get the sand from?' asked Cassie.

'I asked that friendly groundsman for a seed tray and some gravel and sand – I said I wanted to grow some plants indoors.' Becky replied. 'He told me to help myself.'

'Does Tinker know what it's for yet?'

'Yes. He's being very good about using it, thank goodness,' said Becky.

'We'll have to open all the windows and slosh some disinfectant around before Mrs Ramsbottom's inspection tomorrow morning,' said Cassie.

By lunchtime they were dying to know how the boys had been faring with Marmalade. They went straight over to their table and asked them.

'He never keeps still,' grumbled Matthew. 'You only have to sit down for a moment and he's jumped on to your shoulders!'

'Did you keep him hidden all right when your housemaster did his rounds?' asked Cassie.

'Oh yes,' said Tom. 'He was good then. We put him in the wardrobe on one of my jumpers and luckily he went to sleep.'

'There's a terrible pong though,' said Matthew. 'When can you have him back?'

'We don't know,' said Cassie. 'We haven't made a plan yet.'

'Well, don't take too long, will you?' said Matthew.

'Oh, stop moaning,' said Tom. 'I'm really enjoying having Marmers about.'

The children decided to give the kittens (and their rooms) an airing after lunch, smuggling them out into a part of the grounds well away from the school buildings, and letting them have a romp around together.

'I wonder if they've missed each other?' asked Emily.

'They certainly seem to like playing together,' Cassie answered.

Putting the kittens back in their rooms, the children were conscious that they wouldn't be able to go up to them again until four o'clock, when they had their homework period. In fact, they needn't have worried. Both Marmalade and Tinker seemed to have made themselves quite at home.

'I'll just pop round and ask Lesley to look after Tink while we're in detention after supper,' said Poppy.

'Good idea,' said Becky. 'We can give her some scraps to feed him.'

To their surprise, Mitsi, who had been watching Tinker investigate a paper bag, suddenly bent down and stroked his head cautiously.

'Careful, Mitsi,' laughed Poppy. 'You might even get to like him.'

'I do already,' said Mitsi, smiling.

After playing with Tinker when they should have been getting on with their prep, the girls, apart from Becky, who had extra ballet coaching with Miss Waters, made their way to Studio One. They were surprised to find a lot of third year girls already there.

Madame Larette clapped her hands. '*Maintenant!* I 'ave chosen who is going forward to the audition.'

An excited murmur ran round the crowded studio, as she read out the names of eight of the third year girls and then began on the second year list:

'Mitsuko, Celia, Abigail, Jane, Emily, Vanessa . . .'

Cassie's heart was beginning to pound. Surely she would not be left out?

'. . . Cassandra and Poppy,' finished Madame Larette.

Cassie smiled her relief at Poppy.

'I'm sorry some of you 'ave been disappointed tonight, but remember, eight more will 'ave to be disappointed at the audition. Perhaps you girls can go next door now. Miss Oakland is waiting for you, to do some practice en pointe.'

Another surprise was in store for the girls who remained when a few minutes later, Miss Wrench entered the studio. There was an immediate hush, as the girls sank in unison into a deep curtsy.

'Good evening, girls,' she said.

It transpired that she wanted to oversee the rehearsal and help Madame to group the girls according to height. Second and third years couldn't be mixed, which presented a problem for Cassie, as she was the tallest of her year. This left her group, which consisted of herself, Jane, Celia and Vanessa, rather unbalanced. The girls in the other second year group – Emily, Poppy, Abigail and Mitsi – were virtually the same height. Cassie registered the unalterable fact that their group would *look* better. It made her more determined that her own group should dance brilliantly.

As the rehearsal wore on, Cassie threw herself into the work with great energy, exhorting her group to greater efforts. She wished that Celia were not among them, because she couldn't stand working so closely with her.

In the changing-room, Celia was unbearable. She

started bragging to Abigail about how they'd been chosen.

'I knew we'd get through!' she crowed, in full hearing of the girls who hadn't been chosen and who had just come in from Miss Oakland's class. 'Of course, it takes talent. And talent is what you and I have both got, Abi.'

Abigail shrugged, but Cassie couldn't help noticing a self-satisfied smile flit across her face.

As the days went by, Cassie found herself extremely busy, helping to look after Tinker by day and rehearsing every evening for the coming *Swan Lake* audition. There was a great build-up of excitement as the audition came closer, and the girls involved were all beginning to get a little snappy with one another.

It was getting more and more difficult to hide Tinker now, partly because of the catty smell, and partly because he was getting more boisterous and mischievous, especially on days when they couldn't take him outside at all. By the weekend, Cassie felt exhausted and was glad of Saturday afternoon to sit about and do nothing. Becky and Poppy had taken Tinker out to the folly for some fresh air, and Emily and Mitsi had gone off to the village. Thus Cassie found herself deliciously alone and quiet.

But not for long. Celia burst in, unannounced as always, and looked surprised to see that Cassie was the only one in the room.

'Where is everyone?' she asked.

'Oh, here and there,' answered Cassie airily.

Celia gave her a none-too-pleasant smile. Her cat-like eyes made her appear sly when she smiled like that.

'I've been hearing rumours,' she said.

'Oh?'

'That you've got a kitten in here.' She started poking around the room. Cassie was glad she had pushed the cat's litter-tray and bowl under the wardrobe earlier on.

'That's a load of rubbish,' said Cassie. 'Can you just leave me in peace, Celia?'

'Suit yourself,' said Celia, unabashed. 'But you can't keep it secret forever, all the same.'

'Oh, get lost!' shouted Cassie angrily.

As Celia fled, Cassie tried to regain the sense of peace she had felt earlier, but without success. With Celia on the alert, how could they hope to keep Tinker hidden for much longer? She racked her brains for an alternative hiding-place. It was no use asking the boys to hide yet another kitten – they were just about at the end of their tether with Marmalade as it was. Whatever could the girls do with Tinker? They *couldn't* let him be put down, that was certain.

8

Kittens and Cygnets

The girls spent an anxious afternoon, after Cassie had warned them about Celia's visit.

'It's only a matter of time,' said Cassie pacing up and down the room. 'Either Celia will find him and tell Mrs Ramsbottom, or Mrs Ramsbottom will find him herself.'

'And the boys have had enough of Marmalade,' added Emily. 'Their housemaster very nearly caught them red-handed yesterday!'

'It's not ideal keeping them in our rooms anyway,' said Becky. 'Much as I love Tinker, I know he'd be better off with a garden to play in.'

A pretty cottage garden suddenly flashed across

Cassie's mind. Mrs Allingham's garden.

'I've got it!' she cried. 'Put Tinker in your bag, Becky. We're going for a walk!'

'But where?' asked Becky, totally perplexed. The answer dawned on her as they strode across the lawns in the direction of the orchard.

'Mrs Allingham, of course!' cried Becky.

'We'll just have time to get there and back before supper.'

'Oh, I hope she agrees to keep him,' said Becky, crossing her fingers tightly. 'But what about Marmalade?'

'One thing at a time,' said Cassie.

Very soon, an astonished Mrs Allingham was being presented with a black and white kitten, on the doorstep of her cottage.

'He's called Tinker,' said Cassie. 'Would you like him?'

'Oh yes!' said the old lady without hesitation. 'It's years since my cat Jefferson died. It would be so nice to have a new kitten. Come in, come in.'

Tinker seemed to know he had to be on his best behaviour. Cassie had been fearful that he might jump around and break some of Mrs Allingham's many china ornaments or vases. But he obligingly curled up in the old lady's lap, purring loudly.

'Oh, isn't he a dear?' she said, smiling.

Becky looked very relieved that Tinker liked Mrs Allingham, whereas Cassie's concern was more the other way round. She was wondering how to bring up the fact there was a second homeless kitten. It seemed too much to ask of her, to take in *both* kittens.

'A penny for them,' said Mrs Allingham, looking at her intently.

Cassie laughed. 'Oh, I was just thinking.'

'Well, it looked a worried thought. Is it something to do with Tinker?'

Cassie cleared her throat. 'Well yes, sort of.'

She quickly outlined the kittens' story, finishing with the precarious position that Marmalade was still in, under Matthew and Tom's supervision.

'Your new housemother sounds a tartar!' exclaimed Mrs Allingham.

'A tartar!' echoed Becky. 'Yes, I like that description of her.'

'Well,' went on Mrs Allingham, 'you needn't worry for a moment longer, Cassandra. Nor you, Rebecca. For I know how dearly you love animals. Marmalade shall make his home with me ... and Tinker, of course.'

Tinker had chosen that moment to stand up with both paws resting on Mrs Allingham's chest, and lick her chin. Both the girls laughed.

'It's as though he understood you!' said Cassie.

'When shall we bring Marmalade round?' asked Becky.

'By the sound of it, there's not a moment to lose. Why don't you go and fetch him straight away?'

Cassie looked at her watch. 'We'll have to go to supper first. But we could come back right after it.'

Mrs Allingham clicked her teeth reprovingly.

'Now you know as well as I do, that's against the

rules. I'm afraid you'll have to leave it until first thing tomorrow.'

Becky cuddled Tinker and said goodbye to him. Cassie could see she was struggling not to cry.

'Now don't you worry about him, my dear,' said Mrs Allingham. 'You can come to play with him any time you like. It's always lovely to see you.'

The girls thanked Mrs Allingham profusely and ran back to school, to be in time for their supper. Their news was greeted with great relief, not only by their room-mates, but also by Matthew and Tom who were getting decidedly edgy about keeping Marmalade any longer.

'He's chewed all the bottom of my briefcase!' moaned Matthew. 'And the housemaster's getting suspicious.'

'Well, I tell you what,' said Cassie. 'We'll take him back now. We should manage to keep him hidden for just one night.'

Becky brightened instantly. 'I'll come up with my bag and fetch him.'

'Oh, great,' said Matthew. 'What a relief!'

Marmalade enjoyed sniffing around Room Twelve at first, probably smelling Tinker's scent, but he soon became restless and started mewing.

Becky tried to muffle the noise.

'D'you think he's missing Matthew and Tom?' asked Cassie.

'No, more likely he's been reminded of his brother.'

'It's nice that they can be together again soon, isn't it?' said Mitsi.

Ominous footsteps could be heard coming along the landing.

'It's the tartar!' whispered Becky, plunging Marmalade into her large bag, and thrusting it inside the wardrobe.

Mrs Ramsbottom entered without knocking.

'A little bird has told me that you *again* have an animal in your room,' she boomed.

Cassie and Becky exchanged glances. They knew which little bird it was. The girls all shook their heads and tried to look innocent and unconcerned as Mrs Ramsbottom prowled around their room.

Then the thing they had been dreading happened. Marmalade started mewing and scratching at the inside of the wardrobe door, to be let out. Mrs Ramsbottom, with a look of triumph, obliged.

'Yet *another* cat!' she cried. 'This room seems to be turning into a zoo! Well, this time,' she paused, 'I'm making sure the cat is put right into the hands of the caretaker. Then there'll be no more mistakes.'

One by one, the girls dissolved into tears, but this only seemed to harden Mrs Ramsbottom's resolve. She bent down to scoop up the kitten, but, as if sensing her hostility, he bit her hand.

'Ow,' she yelped. 'Cassandra, you'll have to carry him for me.'

'Yes, Mrs Ramsbottom,' said Cassie.

Becky looked at her with grief-stricken eyes. Cassie took a deep breath.

'But not to the caretaker.'

'*What* did you say, you impertinent girl?'

'I said, not to the caretaker. I'll carry him with pleasure to Mrs Allingham's, where he has been offered a good home!'

'I don't know what you're talking about. Do as you're told!'

'No, I refuse,' said Cassie, holding the kitten tightly to her, guessing that Mrs Ramsbottom would not dare reach out for the animal again.

Mrs Ramsbottom was nearly purple with repressed fury. 'Come to Miss Wrench immediately!' she spluttered.

Cassie obeyed instantly; this was just what she had been hoping for. She knew they would all be in trouble for harbouring animals, but she also knew that the Principal would be fair where the kitten was concerned.

Her faith in Miss Wrench turned out to be sound. After a brief telephone call to Mrs Allingham, the Principal turned to the housemother and pupil.

'Mrs Allingham confirms what Cassandra said. She is quite willing to give both kittens a home. So there will be no need to involve the caretaker, I think, Mrs Ramsbottom. Perhaps you would care to leave me to deal with Cassandra now, Mrs Ramsbottom. Oh, and could you ask Rebecca to take the kitten along to Mrs Allingham's cottage?'

'Oh yes, certainly Miss Wrench.' Mrs Ramsbottom left the room, looking far from happy.

'Now Cassandra. I was hoping we would have a term free from incident. But already you are before me, having been rude and disobedient to your housemother.'

86

'I wasn't rude, Miss Wrench,' said Cassie in her own defence. 'I just couldn't take poor Marmalade to be put down. It would have been so cruel!'

The Principal looked thoughtful. 'Well, I do know how attached children get to animals. But you behaved very stupidly, taking the kittens into your room in the first place.'

'Yes, Miss Wrench. I am sorry. We all are.'

'Well, I hope this fright has taught you all a lesson. I shall be taking no further action. But let me make it very clear, if there is any further *hint* of disobedience to Mrs Ramsbottom, you will be in very serious trouble.'

By lunch-time the next day their fears had all been forgotten, when Cassie, Becky, Poppy, Emily and Mitsi all filed into the tiny sitting-room at Mrs Allingham's to watch the two kittens playing happily together.

'It's very nice to meet your new friends,' said Mrs Allingham happily. 'I *am* having a busy week.'

'So are we!' said Cassie. 'The audition's on Thursday.'

'So soon! Well, well. And are you all going in for it?'

'All of us except Becky,' answered Cassie.

'Yes, poor old me,' said Becky. 'I'm still slogging away with the first years. But I didn't want to be in *Swan Lake* anyway. It's a soppy sort of ballet. Swans changing into maidens!'

Mrs Allingham smiled. 'I don't imagine Cassandra agrees with you there.'

'No, I don't,' cried Cassie. 'It's an amazing ballet. And so sad at the end.'

'I don't really know the story,' piped up Mitsi.

'Oh, don't you?' asked Mrs Allingham. 'Well, you know, it was one of the very first ballets to be shown outside Russia, and I'm sure you've heard the beautiful music for it.'

'Yes, by Tchaikovsky, isn't it?' said Mitsi.

'That's right. Prince Siegfried, the hero of the ballet, goes out hunting wild swans and meets a beautiful swan who turns into a girl called Odette. She has been enchanted by the wicked magician, Von Rothbart, and must live as a swan by day, only taking up her human form by night. Odette tells Prince Siegfried she can be saved only if a man swears to love her, and no one else, for ever. Siegfried is happy to do this, as he has fallen in love at first sight, but unfortunately Von Rothbart finds out and sends his daughter, Odile, disguised as Odette, to the Prince's ball the next day. She tricks the Prince into asking her to marry him.'

'Odile always wears black, doesn't she?' added Cassie.

'Yes,' said Mrs Allingham, 'to contrast with the pure white costume of Odette.'

'And does that mean that the spell can't be broken for Odette?' asked Mitsi.

'Well now, I'm coming to that. Poor old Siegfried sees Odette at the window of his palace and rushes to her. The only way they can break the spell, along with the Prince's binding promise to marry Odile, is to plunge into the lake and die together. This, by the way, causes the death of the magician.'

'I see what you mean about the sad ending,' said Mitsi.

'But that's not quite the end,' said Emily. 'You see their spirits carried across the lake on a beautiful swan-shaped boat. It's lovely!'

'Load of old rubbish if you ask me!' Becky cut in.

'Oh Becky, where's your sense of the romantic?' laughed Cassie. 'I can't wait to go to the audition.'

When the day came, it was every bit as exciting as Cassie had dreamed it would be. The girls were picked up from school after lunch in a minibus which took them directly to the Hippodrome. Their audition was squeezed into the break in a rehearsal which meant that they were able to watch a few minutes of the company dancing and, better still, to rub shoulders with some of the Principals in the wings. They had to be ready, as soon as the act under rehearsal was finished.

'Oh, that was Miriam Fenella and Vaslav Orensky!' breathed Cassie as the pair who danced Odette and Siegfried came off stage, so near they could have touched them. 'Weren't they wonderful?'

As the task ahead hit her, Cassie's excitement turned to nervousness. It would be better, she thought, if her group were to be called first. But unluckily, the director called from the darkened auditorium that he wanted to start with the third year groups. Cassie peered from the side of the stage to see if she could make out Robert Weston, the director,

89

or his assistant, but it was too hazy and dark. Madame Larette, who was with the students, pulled her back smartly.

'You cannot see 'im, but 'e can see you!' she warned.

Cassie apologised and watched the two third year groups from the wings, feeling more and more nervous. A few deep breaths helped a little. Then there was a pause, as the director and his assistant, who was the principal ballet mistress with the Birmingham Royal Ballet, went into a huddle.

'They are making their decision,' murmured Madame.

She was right. The ballet mistress called out the names of the first group who had danced, telling them they had been successful.

'Our turn now,' whispered Cassie, with a horrible colly-wobbly feeling going round her stomach.

In fact, Emily's group was called first. As she saw her friends begin the familiar little swans' dance, it struck her again how their heights were almost perfectly matched. But over and above that, their movements were almost perfectly in unison. Cassie swallowed hard. It would be a difficult act to follow. Celia approached her before they stepped on stage.

'I think we've got a good chance,' she said. 'Apart from Abigail, that lot were pretty awful.'

'Don't be stupid, Celia. They were really good, really together,' Cassie retorted. 'By the way, did you tell Mrs Ramsbottom we'd got a kitten in our room?'

'Me?' said Celia grinning. 'Wouldn't dream of it.' She laughed. 'Your lot should learn to obey school rules. Then you wouldn't be getting into trouble all the time.'

Cassie went on to the stage, seething. A rush of adrenaline flooded through her, as the group of four took up their starting position and listened to the opening beats of the music. She put everything she had into the dance, and was only dimly conscious of her partners. At the end, she wondered if they had stayed together – she really couldn't remember.

Another pause. Another huddle. It didn't take very long for the director and his assistant to decide.

'Oh, please let it be our group!' wished Cassie fervently.

But Mr Weston announced that the first group – Emily's group – had been successful in the audition, while complimenting all the dancers on their high level of professionalism.

'There you are,' said Madame, looking pleased. 'A nice compliment for Redwood.'

Cassie couldn't speak. She had never felt so disappointed in the whole of her life. Abigail, Emily, Mitsi and Poppy were hugging one another ecstatically, rather like footballers when a goal has just been scored. Madame had to calm them down.

'Now, girls,' she said with a twinkle in her eye. 'Remember what Mr Weston said about your *professionalism*.'

Emily was the first to notice the state Cassie was in. She slipped an arm around her friend's shoulder. 'I wish you could have been with us,' she said gently.

'You deserved to be chosen,' said Cassie. 'You

danced fantastically.' She gulped down her own feelings of intense disappointment and congratulated Mitsi, Poppy, and, hardest of all, Abigail. A crestfallen Celia joined the group.

'Well, done,' she said to Abigail, but without much enthusiasm. 'That's more than I can say to the rest of you!' she remarked unpleasantly. 'The director must have had his eyes shut.'

Madame was approaching as Celia was still speaking. Her eyes narrowed as she looked at the girl.

'Part of learning to be a dancer is learning to cope with your disappointments,' she said.

Cassie took her words back with her to Redwood. They were the only comfort she had.

9

An Unexpected Opportunity

Cassie was out of spirits the following morning. Her friends noticed at once, as normally she was such a bundle of energy. Becky was especially nice to her, as she was not involved with *Swan Lake* anyway.

'Cheer up, Cassie,' she chivvied. 'Just think of all the extra work the others will have to catch up on.'

Cassie smiled ruefully. 'I wouldn't have minded. I'd have worked my socks off.'

'Well, it just wasn't to be,' said Becky. 'As my mum says, "These things come for a purpose".'

It was some consolation to see what a bad mood Celia was in, when they saw her later in lesson-time. Even in her favourite lesson, maths, with her favourite teacher, Mrs Ramsbottom, she was surly and bad-tempered. Mrs Ramsbottom quickly grew tired of Celia's behaviour and, before the lesson was over, had given her a black mark.

Further consolation was to come from Madame Larette. She took Cassie on one side during their afternoon pointe work class, to discuss the audition with her.

'I know you must be very disappointed, *ma chérie*, but let me tell you, you danced beautifully. If it had been a soloist they were looking for, I 'ave no doubt they would 'ave chosen you, Cassandra.'

Cassie looked at her in surprise. 'So why wasn't our group chosen, then?'

'Two reasons. The main one was that Emily's group, as I'm sure you've noticed, was evenly matched in height, whereas you were noticeably the tallest in your group. The second reason is that your group were – 'ow can I put it – not of one heart.'

The antipathy between her and Celia passed through Cassie's mind, as she nodded and thanked Madame for explaining things to her.

As the days went by, Cassie came to terms with the blow her failure had dealt her. Madame had reassured her that the quality of her dancing was good enough, but she was left with a gnawing anxiety that she was just going to be too tall to become a professional dancer.

Emily, Mitsi, Poppy and Abigail started attending afternoon rehearsals at the Hippodrome, and the twinges of jealously she felt got less and less each time

94

they set off in the minibus. They returned each tea-time, bursting with stories about the professional dancers they were working with and tales about Mr Weston, the director, who was quite eccentric and who had turned up one day to the theatre in a white dinner jacket and red and blue spotty bow-tie. Cassie lapped up all their news, trying her hardest not to feel excluded. She was grateful that Becky stayed at school with her on the afternoons the others were missing.

By coincidence, the 'little swans' managed to miss lots of maths lessons. Cassie and Becky were aware of Mrs Ramsbottom's mounting irritation and weren't at all surprised that she made life as difficult as she could for their other room-mates. Celia was back in favour, and fawning all over Abigail at every available opportunity.

'It's a pity that Abigail can't see through Celia,' Emily remarked one morning.

'Yes,' agreed Cassie. 'But Celia seems to bring out her worst side.'

'It's a shame,' said Poppy. 'She's good fun when she's with us at rehearsals. And not a bit catty, is she, Mitsi?'

'No,' said Mitsi. 'I like Abigail. But I agree with Cassie – when she's with Celia, she's like a different person.'

'Can you believe it's the dress rehearsal tomorrow?' said Emily.

'It's hard to,' agreed Poppy. 'Time seems to have whizzed by!'

Miss Oakland announced in ballet class that the whole of the second and third year were invited to watch the *Swan Lake* dress rehearsal the following day. Cassie had mixed feelings about going, but kept them to herself.

In the end, she enjoyed the performance for the most part. She just sat back and let the beautiful music flood through her body, while her eyes feasted on the delicious dancing and costumes of the Birmingham Royal Ballet company.

Vaslav Orensky and Miriam Fenella, the principals, were brilliant as Odette and Siegfried, and Cassie also loved watching the graceful, swan-like movements of the corps-de-ballet. It was something of a jolt when she saw her friends coming on to the stage for their 'Dance of the Little Swans'. It seemed so out of keeping, somehow, for them to be up there. But she had to admit to herself that they were dancing very well. It was obvious that the rehearsals with Robert Weston had paid off, as their performance looked much more polished and professional now. Cassie would have loved the opportunity of working under Mr Weston – she sensed how much she would have learned.

After the rehearsal, glasses of squash were provided for the youngsters in the audience and they had the chance to wander about the theatre.

'I'll be glad to get back to school,' said Becky. 'I'm bored stiff!'

'Oh, I don't know how you can be,' said Cassie.

'Well, you're not me. I haven't seen Tinker for the

past two days, 'cause I had to go to my cello lesson in the lunch hour yesterday. Then we didn't have much time today.'

'I shouldn't worry,' said Cassie. 'He and Marmalade seem awfully happy with Mrs Allingham. In fact they couldn't have found a better home.'

'Oh, I know,' agreed Becky. 'I don't *worry* about him. I just miss him.'

'Well, it's all turned out really well. We can see Tinker nearly every day *and* Mrs Allingham's less lonely too.'

'I wonder which dressing-room the girls are in?' said Becky suddenly.

'Shall we be cheeky and try to find them?' asked Cassie.

After asking a few dancers they met in the backstage corridors, they were directed to the small dressing-room where Emily, Mitsi, Poppy and Abigail were changing. They were surprised to find Celia already there, fussing around Abigail. Emily seemed very quiet, which seemed odd, Cassie thought, after such an exciting occasion.

'That was great!' said Cassie enthusiastically.

'Yeh,' said Becky, not quite as convincingly.

Poppy was bubbling over with high spirits, while Abigail and Celia chattered excitedly to each other. But Emily and Mitsi were both subdued. It wasn't until Becky and Cassie got them on their own much later that they discovered what had upset them.

'It was Celia,' said Emily.

'Might have guessed,' said Becky, sniffing.

'She came into our dressing-room and started asking us all if our parents were coming to watch any of the performances.'

'That wasn't very tactful,' said Cassie. 'For a start, she knows jolly well that Mitsi's and Poppy's parents are on the other side of the world.'

A tear trickled down Mitsi's cheek. 'I've spoken to them on the phone and they're so pleased I'm in *Swan Lake*, but they just can't take time off work to come and see me.'

'Never mind,' said Becky. 'I'm sure they're thinking of you.'

'I do miss them so,' sniffed Mitsi.

'But Celia couldn't have known about your dad, Em, surely?' asked Cassie.

'*She* seems to get to know everything about everybody,' cried Emily. 'I'm sure she did know something, because she just kept pressing me to say which night my dad was coming to watch.'

'How awful for you!' said Cassie. 'What did you say?'

'I had to end up telling her Mum and Dad were separated and I didn't know if Dad would come or not.'

Cassie squeezed Emily's hand. She knew how much her friend hated talking about her family's problems.

The next day, Emily at least seemed to have recovered her composure, until another unfortunate meeting with Celia in the changing-room before morning ballet class.

'Oh, here's the girl who doesn't know where her father's got to!' sneered Celia as Emily walked past her.

Emily stopped dead. Cassie saw her face turn as white as chalk and her hands clench into fists. But before Cassie could spring to her friend's defence, she was surprised to find that Abigail had already turned on Celia.

'That's a really *horrible* thing to say, Celia!' she said. 'If that's what you're like to people, I don't want to have anything more to do with you!'

It was obvious from Celia's face that nothing Cassie could have said would have had a tenth of the effect of Abigail's remark. But Emily was still terribly upset at having her father's disappearance paraded in public.

'Don't worry about it, Emily,' Cassie said, drawing her to one side. 'We're all on your side – except Celia of course. Nobody will think any the less of you, can't you see that?'

'You can't understand how it feels,' murmured Emily. 'It's a kind of guilty feeling.'

'It's not your fault,' urged Cassie. 'Your dad went for his own reasons. You musn't blame yourself.'

Even the usual orderly calm of ballet class didn't last on that particular day. Ten minutes into barre exercises, Madame was just demonstrating how the girls could improve their battements frappés, when Mrs Ramsbottom strode in. Madame looked up in surprise. She had taken over the class from Miss Oakland, who had flu.

'Oh, Mrs Ramsbottom!' she said. 'Is there some emergency?'

The class looked on, expectantly.

'No, no,' answered Mrs Ramsbottom. She was plainly very angry. 'I'd just like to know how these second years who keep nipping off to the Hippodrome can be expected to keep up with their mathematics?'

Madame looked bemused.

'They have missed six lessons so far this term,' went on Mrs Ramsbottom loudly. 'And now I'm informed that they are to miss yet *more* when they dance in matinées!'

'Well, I don't quite see why . . .' began Madame.

'I came to you, because you're principal ballet mistress. Perhaps you could put a stop to this . . . this *nonsense*!'

'I couldn't possibly stop them dancing in *Swan Lake* now,' said an astonished Madame. 'And really, if you object to the principle of their taking part in productions, you should speak to Miss Wrench.'

'I shall, don't worry, I shall,' boomed Mrs Ramsbottom, as she stormed out of the studio.

Madame Larette seemed flustered for the rest of the class and hurried off as soon as the students had curtsyed to her.

'Off to see Miss Wrench, I shouldn't wonder,' said Cassie.

Lunch was a miserable affair. Mitsi couldn't stop thinking about her parents, Emily was still upset from her brush with Celia, and Cassie was generally depressed about not being a little swan. But then news reached their ears of an argument in the Principal's study, which had been overheard by a couple of third year boys. In no time at all, the dining-hall was throbbing with the information that Miss Wrench and Mrs Ramsbottom had had a blazing row. It lifted the friends' spirits tremendously.

Mr Green, who was on dinner-duty, came over to Cassie's table, when they were guessing who had come off worse.

'I've a message for you, Cassandra,' he said, frowning. 'And could you girls please refrain from *gossiping*.'

'Who's it from?' asked Cassie in surprise.

'Mrs Allingham,' said Mr Green. 'She wants to see you as soon as possible.'

'Oh thank you, Mr Green,' said Cassie. As he walked away, she looked at Becky.

'You don't think something's wrong, do you?'

Becky looked worried. 'Oh, if anything's happened to Tinker!'

'Well, there's one way to find out,' said Cassie. 'Let's go straight away.'

She, Becky and Emily ran all the way to the little ivy-covered cottage and knocked on the door as if their lives depended on it.

'All right, all right,' said Mrs Allingham, smiling as she opened the door. 'Don't knock it down!'

She took in their anxious faces. 'Oh, I hope I haven't worried you with my message. The kittens are fine!'

The girls could see that for themselves as soon as they went into her sitting-room. Tinker and Marmalade were both curled up contentedly on the rug in front of a glowing log fire. Seeing Becky come

101

into the room, Tinker padded across to her and rubbed his head against her leg. Becky soon had him in her arms and Emily quickly followed suit with Marmalade.

'While those two are occupied with the cats,' said Mrs Allingham to Cassie, 'I can tell you the good news.'

'Good news?'

'Yes, I'm sure you'll think so. The director of Northern Ballet – a very dear friend of mine – phoned me yesterday in a bit of a state. He's putting on a production of *The Nutcracker* for the Christmas season in Birmingham and one of his Claras has broken her leg. They have to have two, you know, who take it in turns. It's too much for one child to appear in every performance.'

Cassie looked puzzled.

'So he's frantic – he's got to find another Clara at very short notice and hasn't got time to go through the usual procedure of advertising and auditioning in the north. He asked me if I could recommend anyone.'

Cassie began to understand. Her eyes lit up.

'I've had a word with Miss Wrench and she gives her approval for you to audition for the part.'

'Oh, that's wonderful, Mrs Allingham!' Cassie cried, throwing her arms around the old lady's neck. 'How can I ever thank you?'

'Now, you haven't got the part yet, Cassandra,' Mrs Allingham said, checking her. 'Miss Wrench is going to put forward two other girls – Jane and Celia, I think she said. All the other likely candidates are already in *Swan Lake*, I believe.'

Cassie's excitement abated a little. But she still knew she stood a very good chance, as long as she didn't do anything stupid. She couldn't wait to talk to her mum and dad about it on the phone. That very night was the first performance of *Swan Lake*, and she waved Emily, Mitsi, Poppy and Abigail off in the minibus, without the slightest feeling of jealousy. Soon perhaps she would be going off like them. If only she could dance really well at the audition!

When she phoned her parent, they were thrilled, as they'd guessed how disappointed Cassie had been about not getting chosen for the little swans. Her mum decided to come down for the audition at the Hippodrome the following Friday, as she could take Cassie home with her after it for the half-term holiday.

The atmosphere was quite different this time in the theatre. The company were not around – their rehearsal was already over. The stage and wings seemed big and empty and, as Cassie stepped forward, she was glad that her mother stood in the wings, so close to her.

The director – Fred Gibbings – introduced himself. Cassie could only make him out dimly, as the stage lights dazzled her, but his voice came over loud and clear.

'So you're June's young friend,' he boomed. 'Cassandra Brown, isn't it?'

'Yes, that's right, Mr Gibbings.'

'Well, let's see what you can do, Cassandra. I believe

you're going to dance your last exam set piece for us?'

Cassie agreed. She nodded to the pianist, who had accompanied the girls from Redwood, and took up her starting pose. She danced carefully, paying attention to each detail of foot, head and hand position. It was not the sort of dance, however, in which you could show any character. There had been no time to learn anything specially for the audition.

Joy, Cassie's mum, hugged her warmly, as she rushed off stage, after being thanked by Mr Gibbings. 'You danced wonderfully,' she said.

Together, they watched Jane's and Celia's dances. Jane had had to do the same piece as Cassie, for want of anything else. Cassie knew, however, watching her, that Jane wasn't doing herself justice. Celia had the advantage of knowing a different solo piece, from her previous school, which although somewhat simpler, was more dramatic and expressive. She knew that acting was just as important as dancing in Clara's role and Celia had conveyed the character of her piece very effectively.

'I don't know *what* I'll do if Celia gets this part,' she whispered to her mum, as Mr Gibbings was thanking Celia.

'I do,' said Joy. 'Go on dancing!'

'Oh, Mum,' said Cassie. 'It can't slip through my fingers again!'

Fred Gibbings conferred with his assistant for a few unbearably long minutes. Then came a surprise request.

'Cassandra and Celia – could you both go to dressing-room ten and slip on the Clara costumes the dresser's got ready for you? Come back up here as soon as you've changed.'

Again, Cassie was glad of her mother's presence, this time to act as a buffer between her and Celia. The wardrobe mistress handed each of the girls a long, loose pink nightdress, with frills at the neck and cuffs.

'There's not much problem about fitting with these,' she remarked to Joy. 'And luckily they're not too long.' She explained that this was the costume Clara wore when she came back downstairs late at night after her family's party was over.

'I wonder what Mr Gibbings wants us to do now?' said Cassie to her mum.

'Soon find out!'

Back on stage, the girls were asked, in turn, to run freely around the stage, and then to mime their reactions to seeing an army of mice coming into their living-room. Cassie went on second and, when she joined her mother again, her heart was throbbing with the thrill of it all. If she got the part, she inwardly promised, she would be nice to everyone in the whole world – even Celia and Mrs Ramsbottom. Cassie, Celia and Jane waited together at the side of the stage for Mr Gibbings's decision. Jane had already changed into her outdoor clothes, ready for the return to Redwood.

'Well, it's all over for me anyway,' Jane said, sighing.

Although she was anxious about the outcome of Fred Gibbings's deliberations, Cassie still felt sympathetic to Jane's disappointment. 'Bad luck,

Jane!' she said. 'But you danced really well.' Cassie stared intently into the auditorium. Not that she could see very much. She was startled when Mr Gibbings called Celia's name. Celia! Cassie looked at her mother with a stricken expression. Joy Brown stroked her daughter's head, as Celia rushed forward.

'Oh, there you are,' said Mr Gibbings. 'And what about Jane? Is she in the wings too?'

Jane came forward shyly, to join Celia on the stage.

'Thank you, girls, for attending today. I've enjoyed watching you both, but I don't need to keep you any longer. You can have a look around the theatre until your lift is due.'

Cassie listened with a pounding heart. Could this really mean she was the one who was to be chosen?

'You've got it, Cassie!' whispered her mum. 'You've got it!'

10

Red Roses for Emily

Mr Gibbings invited Cassie and her mother down to where he was sitting to discuss dates of performances and Cassie's fees.

'I didn't expect to get paid for it!' Cassie said later, on their way back to school.

'It's a professional engagement,' said her mother. 'It's only fair you get paid. It'll give a nice boost to your piggy bank.'

'I can hardly believe it all!' cried Cassie, and was going to say more when she caught sight of Jane's and Celia's glum faces. She stayed quiet for the rest of the journey.

'Are you free to come home now?' asked Joy, as

they pulled up in the school drive. Cassie consulted her watch.

'No, we've still got character class. I'll have to go to that but I can leave at six-thirty without supper.'

'That's fine,' said Joy. 'I'll nip back into the city and do some shopping and come back for you later. I think we should have your favourite supper to celebrate.'

'Good. I'm ravenous already.'

When Joy picked her up at just after half-past six, Cassie was beside herself with excitement. She'd had a chance by then to talk to her friends about her success, and it all seemed so much more real.

Half-term passed in a haze of daydreams and expectations. By the end of the week, Cassie was champing at the bit to get back to ballet school. The weekend she got back, she was surprised to find that not everyone was in such good spirits as she was. Mitsi and Poppy had had to stay at school over the holiday, which hadn't done Poppy any harm, but had redoubled Mitsi's homesickness.

'Oh, it's been so lonely here!' Mitsi exclaimed as all her room-mates returned. 'Thank heavens Poppy was here with me or I'd have gone mad!'

'It must have been tough not having a break from the rotten old place,' Becky said. 'Mum practically had to drag me away from Hammy and Belle.'

'Who's Belle?' asked Cassie. 'Another mouse?'

'No, Mum got me a kitten, when I told her how much I was missing Tinker.'

'Oh, lovely,' said Cassie. 'What's it like?'

'Smoky grey, very fluffy and blue-eyed,' answered

Becky, with adoration in her voice. 'Did either of you get across to see Tinker and Marmalade, by the way?'

'Yes,' replied Poppy. 'We both went twice – it was a welcome change from an empty school, I can tell you, with just Mrs Ramsbottom for company.'

'I bet!' said Cassie. She turned to Emily, who had been noticeably quiet. 'Did you have a good half-term, Em?' she asked.

Emily shrugged. 'Not great,' she said. Cassie knew not to press her in front of everyone, but asked her if she was all right when they were together the next morning in the bathroom.

'I'm OK,' said Emily. 'But it's so depressing at home.'

'Is your mum feeling upset?' asked Cassie.

'She's worn down by the worry and by not having enough money all the time. Where on earth has Dad got to? And why did he have to go?'

'Everything will turn out all right eventually,' said Cassie. It seemed a very inadequate thing to say, but Emily seemed better just for talking about her troubles.

Their room-mates were frantically sorting out Room Twelve when they got back to it.

'I wish I'd put all my stuff away last night!' complained Becky. 'I'd forgotten about Monday morning inspections.'

Emily and Cassie joined in the tidy-up operation and soon all was orderly. When Mrs Ramsbottom came in, she sniffed suspiciously about the room, as though expecting another animal to be lurking somewhere in the undergrowth of uniforms.

After her inspection, she fixed her eyes on Cassie.

'I hear you're another one who's going to be hopping in and out of school!' she said.

'Yes, that's right, Mrs Ramsbottom.'

'Well, I just hope you don't miss too many of *my* lessons. You're behind as it is.'

Cassie fervently wished the opposite, as Mrs Ramsbottom turned to Becky.

'A message for you, Rebecca,' she said abruptly. 'Your progress has been deemed satisfactory and you are to re-join the second year for ballet class from today.'

Becky looked delighted, but needless to say, Mrs Ramsbottom did not. The act of bringing good news was a tiresome task for her.

The friends began to dread going to her maths lessons as, whenever the 'little swans' were there she made them miserable for missing other classes, and when they were absent, she berated the others, especially Cassie, for being so silly as to imagine dancing on stage could prepare you for life half as well as learning maths.

Miss Oakland, too, was in a bad mood with them most of the time, as their major exam approached. Their ballet classes rang to the sound of her raised voice, usually launched with great sarcasm against whichever unfortunate girl she happened to be looking at.

'I wish I were back with the first years,' moaned Becky, after one particularly gruelling lesson. 'At least we weren't shouted at all the time.'

'Miss Oakland leaves you alone,' said Cassie, ''cause you're not taking the exam; so don't complain.'

'Oh, it's our first night tonight,' said Emily with a shiver. 'I can't believe it's come round so quickly.'

'Nor me,' said Poppy.

Abigail popped her head round the corner of the changing-room fixture. 'Are you excited?' she asked.

Cassie half expected to see Celia at her shoulder, like a shadow, but then remembered that Abigail had fallen out with her. Celia was being spiteful to almost everyone now, especially after the disappointment at *The Nutcracker* audition.

As her friends chattered around her about the coming *Swan Lake* performance, Cassie nursed a warm glow inside her: she too had a first night to look forward to.

The 'little swans' first night was swiftly followed by their second, after which they would have a week's rest from performances. Everything had gone very well. Already Emily's mum and Abigail's parents had been to watch their daughters at the Hippodrome.

The morning after the second performance, Emily shook Cassie awake. She had been asleep when the minibus had brought her friends back, late, from the theatre.

'Oh, what is it?' groaned Cassie.

'I've got something really exciting to tell you!' cried Emily, shaking her even harder.

'What?' asked Cassie, sitting up at last, bleary-eyed and resentful.

'Well, last night, when *Swan Lake* finished, one of the theatre staff knocked on our dressing-room door, asking for Emily Pickering.'

'And?' Cassie prompted, interested now.

'Haven't you noticed anything?' asked Emily.

Cassie scrutinised her friend, but gave up.

'Look round the room,' suggested Emily.

'Flowers!' Cassie exclaimed, catching sight of a bouquet of scarlet roses which stood in a bucket of water on Emily's chest of drawers.

'That's right,' said Emily. 'They were delivered to me.'

'How wonderful!' shrieked Cassie. 'Was there a message with them?'

'No, none,' said Emily. 'It's *so* mysterious. Who do you think could have sent them, Cassie?'

Cassie pondered for a long moment. 'Perhaps you've got a secret admirer like Celia.'

The other girls burst out laughing.

'It couldn't be a trick, surely?' said Emily, her face falling.

'An expensive trick,' said Cassie. 'Red roses don't come cheap. No, whoever sent them is genuine, I'm sure.'

The pleasure flooded back into Emily's face.

'You'll have to watch out for any of the boys taking a special interest in you,' said Poppy.

As the week went by, whilst the bouquet wilted, the mystery surrounding it did not. The friends spent every spare minute discussing Emily's possible admirers. She thrived on all the attention. Cassie had never seen her so glowingly happy. But then Cassie became caught up with her own rehearsals for *The Nutcracker*, which at first were small affairs with just her and the principals and Fred Gibbings, as everyone else knew their parts already. She met the other Clara at the second rehearsal. Her name was Katrina Gray and she proved very helpful in teaching Cassie the role. Speed was essential – Cassie was the only member of the cast who was still learning – and she felt the pressure of this, despite Mr Gibbings's laid-back manner. How different he was from the director of the Birmingham Royal Ballet, thought Cassie. Fred Gibbings often turned up in ripped jeans, with his hair looking as though it hadn't seen a comb for days.

Very soon, Cassie got the hang of where she fitted into *The Nutcracker*. There were thirty-nine children altogether in the production, most of whom were students at a ballet school in Manchester. They played the child guests at the Christmas party in Act One, the toy soldiers and the mice. The ballet opened with the Christmas party at the Stahlbaum family's house. Clara and her brother Fritz were joined by many young friends and their parents, but the highlight of the scene was when the mysterious Drosselmeyer – an old man with a patch over his eye – arrived with his presents. Out of three enormous boxes stepped two mechanical dolls and a toy soldier. But the best present – a wooden nutcracker doll – was given to Clara. Fritz became jealous and broke the Nutcracker.

113

Clara's tears were dried by Drosselmeyer and she placed her best-loved toy in a doll's bed under the Christmas tree.

After bedtime, Clara crept back to the sitting-room, where the toys came to life and the seven-headed king of the mice and his army rushed in. Clara helped the nutcracker doll and the toy soldiers to fight the mice, finally defeating their king by throwing a shoe at him.

The Nutcracker, transformed into a prince, took Clara through swirling snowflakes to the Kingdom of Sweets. They were welcomed by the Sugar Plum Fairy and offered a table loaded with sweets. Then the celebrations began. First came a lively Spanish dance, 'Hot Chocolate', followed by a languid Arabian solo, 'Coffee'. 'Tea' was next – a Chinese dance for a boy and two girls. Following this was a rousing Russian peasant *trepak*, and then a dainty, colourful dance by the marzipan shepherdesses. Next came Mother Ginger wearing an enormous hoop skirt, which she drew aside to let out eight children to perform a lively dance. When they had finished, they ran back under Mother Ginger's skirt.

The final part of the entertainment was the lovely 'Waltz of the Flowers' and the pas de deux of the Sugar Plum Fairy and her Nutcracker Prince.

At last, Clara fell asleep and woke up once more on her sitting-room floor, with the toys, now no longer alive, beside her.

Cassie worked very closely with the principal dancing the Nutcracker Prince. His name was Anton

Redowsky and he had been trained at the Kirov in Russia. A little confused by his heavy accent at first, Cassie soon grew to like and respect him. He was always courteous and helpful and never once made her feel she was only a student, however many mistakes she made.

Petronella Finn, the prima ballerina of the company, was dancing the role of the Sugar Plum Fairy, but Cassie had much less to do with her. She stayed in awe of the ballerina, gazing at her in admiration when she danced her solo, or the pas de deux with Anton, but staying tongue-tied on the few occasions when Petronella spoke to her.

Cassie didn't meet the boy playing Fritz straight away. In the earliest rehearsals she had to pretend to squabble and tussle over the nutcracker doll on her own, which seemed quite silly. So, at first, she was relieved when the boy, Andrew, turned up for rehearsals. But Cassie very quickly grew tired of him. She had never met such a spoiled, namby-pamby creature in all her life. His mother hardly ever left his side, and he was to be heard whining and moaning to her at every opportunity. He was not at all popular with the other children in the cast, whereas Cassie fitted in happily, and, where she had half-expected jealousy, she found acceptance and good humour.

Cassie's life felt busier than it had ever been but she still managed to find time at school to go along with Becky and Emily to Mrs Allingham's to play with the kittens a couple of times. Tinker and Marmalade had grown so much that Cassie found it hard to think back to what they were like when she had first seen them at the folly.

After one exhausting rehearsal, Cassie got back to Redwood before her friends, who were doing their third performance of *Swan Lake*. They alternated with the set of third years who had also been chosen as little swans.

Becky was already asleep, and Cassie felt so tired that she was unable to keep herself awake. When Poppy and Mitsi came in at eleven o'clock, she woke with a start.

They were chattering excitedly.

'It's such a mystery!' cried Mitsi.

'What is?' asked Cassie, sitting up, suddenly wide awake.

'You'll never guess!' said Poppy. 'Emily's had another bouquet!'

'Where is she?' asked Cassie.

'Getting a bucket of water from the bathroom.'

The door opened as she spoke, revealing Emily with a bucketful of red roses.

'Aren't they beautiful!' Emily exclaimed. 'I'd never been given flowers before *Swan Lake*. It must have brought me luck.'

'You've certainly won someone's admiration!' said Cassie. 'And why not? You're a star dancer!'

Emily stroked the soft petals of one of the blooms. 'I can't understand why there's no message with the flowers.'

'Same as last time,' Cassie said.

'Oh, whoever is it that's sending them?' Emily burst out.

Becky turned over in bed groaning. 'Be quiet, you lot!' she grumbled.

'It makes it more exciting!' whispered Cassie, 'not knowing.'

'You don't think it could be one of the boys do you?' Mitsi asked.

'I don't think so,' said Poppy, laughing. 'They'd never be able to afford so many flowers.'

'No, of course not,' said Cassie.

Emily sighed. 'Perhaps I'll never find out who sent them! It would be such a waste, though.'

'Just enjoy it,' said Cassie. 'It's been worth it just to see Mrs Ramsbottom's face each time you've had a new bunch. You can tell she hates flowers.'

'And children,' moaned Emily. 'She's been vile to us for missing her lessons.'

'Luckily I've managed to avoid missing maths so far,' said Cassie. 'But that's going to change tomorrow. It's the dress rehearsal, and I'll miss double maths.'

'Watch out then,' said Becky. 'The tartar will be on the warpath.'

The dress rehearsal began at three. Cassie was taken by taxi to the Hippodrome, and made her way to the dressing-room she shared with the other girls. She felt very excited about seeing everyone's costumes.

When she opened the door of the dressing-room, it was packed with girls, wearing either pretty party dresses or mouse costumes. She spotted Katrina Gray

– the other Clara – in the far corner and waved to her. She thought how boring it would be for her today, just watching. Cassie was to be given the chance to dance Clara at the dress rehearsal today, as Katrina had already had that opportunity in Manchester.

Cassie squeezed into a small space and, finding her party costume on a hanger, changed into it. It was the first time she had worn it to dance in and she thought how lovely it was, wishing party dresses still looked so nice. It was a delicate lavender colour, with a pin-tucked bodice, puffed short sleeves and a full skirt with a wide ribbon sash. As soon as she was ready, she went along to the make-up artist, leaving the other girls to the scrum of the dressing-room. Once foundation had been applied quite thickly, Cassie's bone structure was highlighted, her eyebrows and lashes darkened, blusher applied to her cheeks and a vermilion lipstick to her mouth.

She groaned inwardly as Andrew walked in with his mother.

'Here we are, Andrew,' said the make-up lady. 'I've just finished with Cassie, so sit you down.'

As Cassie moved over to the hairdresser, she heard Andrew giving instructions about how his face was to be made up. She tried hard not to giggle.

'And *don't* put that blue eyeshadow on my eyes!' went on Andrew. 'Can't you see my eyes are green?'

'Now, now, Andrew,' soothed his mother. 'Don't get yourself all upset.'

Andrew pouted, which made it very difficult for the lady to apply lipstick to his lips.

'Come on, Andrew,' she coaxed. 'Give me a nice smile.'

'Shan't,' said Andrew, snatching the lipstick from her. 'My mother will do it. She's got more idea than you.'

By now, the hairdresser had caught up Cassie's hair in ribbons and coaxed it into ringlets.

'You've got a lovely natural curl,' she said admiringly. 'There – you look the prettiest Clara I've ever seen.'

Ignoring Andrew's hostile stare, Cassie gazed at herself in the mirror, when the transformation was complete. It looked like someone else, but there were her own brown eyes staring out from the mirror.

For the first time, it really hit Cassie that she was going to dance Clara the following week. A delicious sense of importance flooded through her. She was not just going to be one of the guests, or one of the toys, or one of the mice. She was going to be *Clara*!

She did a quick twirl, to see how her dress would flare out. It looked beautiful, as did her nightdress costume. Cassie could hardly wait for her first night, when her parents and the rest of the audience would see her début.

The dress rehearsal brought her back down to earth with a bump. Fred Gibbings's patience seemed to have suddenly worn thin. No one could do anything right for him, it seemed.

Cassie went through the Christmas party scene anxiously. The other children got into a terrible muddle in their dance as the guests and Fred ended up speaking sharply to them, which was most unusual. Then Andrew, alias Fritz, wrong-footed Cassie in their tussle over the nutcracker doll, causing her to stumble.

When he'd ascertained that Cassie was unhurt, Fred Gibbings launched a tirade at Andrew, which quickly reduced him to tears.

'No point snivelling!' yelled Fred. 'This is our last chance to get it right.'

Instead of making up his mind to do better, as the other children had, Andrew chose that moment to have a full-scale tantrum.

'It's not fair!' he shouted back, stamping his foot. 'You're just picking on me. Why don't you shout at her?' He jabbed a finger in Cassie's direction.

Cassie felt terribly embarrassed to be drawn into the argument, but Fred ignored Andrew's comment.

'Stop being such a baby, and let's go on with the scene, Andrew,' he ordered.

But Andrew had no intention of finishing his tantrum just yet. He continued to wail and mutter until his mother appeared from the wings to comfort him. She turned to face the front row of the auditorium where Fred Gibbings sat.

'I don't know who you think you are,' she said, 'but you have no right to upset Andrew like this. I'm taking him back to the hotel immediately. He's in no state to carry on.'

'But madam,' cried Fred, tearing his hair, 'this is the dress rehearsal! It's essential . . .'

'You should have thought of that before you upset my son. We've had enough. I'm pulling Andrew out of this production. Good afternoon.'

There was a stunned silence as she marched a still-tearful Andrew off the stage. Fred Gibbings looked about him helplessly.

His assistant whispered something to him, before he turned to the cast.

'Is Peter Donaldson on stage?' he asked.

A fair-haired boy, whom Cassie liked, stepped forward.

'Ah, Peter. Do you know Fritz's part?'

'Yes, Mr Gibbings, I think so.' Peter's eyes lit up.

'Could you manage it, d'you think? You're only going to get one practice!'

'I'll try, Mr Gibbings.'

When they started the dress rehearsal once more, from the very beginning, Cassie found Peter much easier to work with than Andrew. Now the crisis had passed, Fred was calmer and everything seemed to go like clockwork. The rest of the rehearsal passed without incident.

Back in the dressing-room, Katrina Gray approached Cassie as she was changing.

'Well done,' she said in a friendly tone. 'You looked as though you'd been dancing Clara all your life.'

Cassie smiled at her. 'Thanks, Katrina. And thank you for all your help.'

'When you've finished getting dressed, I've got a surprise for you,' said Katrina, smiling mysteriously.

'Oh, what? Tell me now!'

'Wait and see.'

Cassie changed quickly, then Katrina led her

through a backstage corridor to the door of another dressing-room.

'Look,' she said proudly. A card on the door read:

CLARA
Katrina Gray   Cassandra Brown

Katrina flung open the door to reveal a small, but very pretty, dressing-room. 'It's just for us!' she said.

'Oh, isn't it lovely!' Cassie breathed, gazing about the room. She tried out the padded revolving chair in front of the mirror. Now she felt like a real star!

'Mr Gibbings wanted us to mix with the other girls during rehearsals,' explained Katrina, 'but for the performances, he said we'd need a little peace and quiet.'

Cassie began to understand what he meant when the big night came. As she sat in the make-up room, she felt very jittery, and hardly glanced at herself when her hair and make-up were finished. She raced back to the dressing-room, eager to put on her costume, and was ready far too early, with nothing to do. She was glad not to be in the overcrowded girls' dressing-room any more, but all she could do now was think about the approaching performance. Katrina had danced Clara the previous evening in the actual first performance of the run. But now it really was Cassie's first night. A shiver ran down her spine. Her family and Becky would already be climbing into their seats in the circle. There would be a big audience. Full house, she had been told. She felt very small and frightened.

Anton found her sitting on the floor, with her head on her knees.

'What's ze matter, my leetle Clara?' he asked gently. He soon had her chuckling at his jokes and, when it was time for curtain-up, he led her by the hand to her starting position.

'Good luck!' he whispered.

Once the curtain had lifted, and the music begun, Cassie felt full of confidence and power, as Anton had promised she would. She threw herself into the part of Clara so fully she could imagine that the magical story was actually happening to her. She gasped in delight at the clockwork toys and argued fiercely over her beloved nutcracker doll. In the transformation scene, she ran and skipped happily with Anton, the Nutcracker Prince, through the twirling snowflakes and then rode proudly with him in a sparkling chariot to the Kingdom of Sweets. There, she could sit back and relax while others danced for her. And then, right at the end, she enjoyed her final moments of glory, alone on the stage, as Clara found herself home once more.

The curtain came down to tumultuous applause. So this was what dancing in a real ballet was like! As Anton led her forward to take her curtsy, Cassie wanted this moment to last forever.

As Becky had come along with the Brown family to share Cassie's first night, she also claimed a share in the big box of chocolates that Joy gave her daughter.

'Delicious!' Becky murmured appreciatively, as she bit into a hazelnut surprise in the theatre bar.

'Yes, I thought she was too,' said Jake Brown, squeezing Cassie's hand.

'Don't be silly, Dad,' said Cassie, embarrassed. 'She meant the chocolate.'

Jake and Joy laughed. Adam, however, scowled into his glass of orange and Cassie couldn't help wishing it could have been her sister Rachel who had come to watch her, not her brother, who didn't like ballet anyway.

'Do you want a chocolate?' she asked Adam suddenly. After all, she had had a perfect night. She could afford to be generous.

'Thanks,' he said, his scowl lifting for a moment.

'Well, Cassie,' said her mum, 'you did marvellously, you really did. I'm so proud of you!'

'Thanks, Mum. I'd better go and get this grease paint off before the taxi arrives.'

Becky grinned. 'She'll be getting too important to speak to us soon.'

Cassie laughed at Becky's joke, never thinking that it might contain an element of truth.

11

An Ultimatum

Without noticing the change in herself, Cassie became so absorbed in her work with the Northern Ballet over the next week or two that everything else began to suffer.

Her friends were the first to notice, of course. Cassie was short-tempered with them and often, in the middle of conversations, she would be silent, with a faraway look in her eyes. When Becky asked her if she wanted to go and see the kittens, she refused. She had lost interest in them. Becky and the others loyally visited Tinker and Marmalade, even though they were obviously very happily settled in Mrs Allingham's cottage. Cassie forgot to practise her violin and got behind with her homework.

The teachers made allowances for her, realising she would be under strain, and her time more limited. All except Mrs Ramsbottom. Mrs Ramsbottom wouldn't let anyone get away with anything. She soon picked on Cassie's untidiness in Room Twelve and talked to her quite severely about it. Then Cassie fell behind with maths work – she should have copied up the work she'd missed, but hadn't. She hadn't even attempted several pieces of homework which Mrs Ramsbottom had set the second year group.

'This really won't do!' Mrs Ramsbottom declared in the maths lesson. 'Cassandra, *all* this work must be handed in by lunch-time tomorrow, or you'll be in very serious trouble.'

'But, Mrs Ramsbottom . . .'

'Yes?'

'I've a performance tonight and . . .'

'I don't care what you've got tonight, Cassandra,' bellowed Mrs Ramsbottom. 'This has gone on long enough.'

'But . . .'

'Tomorrow lunch-time without fail!'

Becky caught up with Cassie after the lesson.

'What are you going to do?' she asked.

Cassie shrugged. 'I've got homework period, but that's all. I'll never get it all done in time. Well, too bad. She shouldn't expect me to do it.'

Becky looked at her. 'I should be careful if I were you,' she said.

126

'Don't be daft, Becky,' snapped Cassie. 'She can only put me in detention. I'm used to those, thanks to her. Anyone else would have taken my special circumstances into consideration.'

Becky was growing a little tired of hearing about her friend's 'special circumstances', but was too kind-hearted to say so.

'Couldn't you take your maths with you tonight? You could do it in the interval, or while you're waiting for the start.'

Cassie gave her a withering look. 'I don't think you understand the pressures of performance, Rebecca. I'm in no state to think about maths when I'm waiting for curtain up!'

'Come on, Becky,' said Abigail, who had come up behind them and overheard the last remark, 'let's leave the prima ballerina to her artistic temperament and go and grab a bun.'

Cassie turned on her. 'Sarcasm is the lowest form of wit, you know. You just don't appreciate what it's like playing such a major role as Clara. I mean, dancing a little swan is just teeny by comparison.'

'There she goes again,' said Abigail. 'Race you to the bun queue!' she shouted at Becky, who quickly took up the challenge, leaving Cassie alone and a little hurt.

They don't understand, she thought. It's beyond them. An anxious feeling about her maths work came over her, but she quickly pushed it down, far down, where it couldn't trouble her.

The next morning she treated her room-mates to a

lengthy description of how the previous night's performance had gone.

'I don't think Petronella was quite on form, though, in the Sugar Plum Fairy solo,' she ended.

'Oh, really, how interesting,' drawled Poppy. The sarcasm was lost on Cassie, who immediately launched into an equally lengthy account of Anton Redowsky's dancing career so far.

'And he thought working in England was the most exciting thing he'd ever done!' she announced.

'You're sure it wasn't meeting you?' Becky joked.

Cassie's self-importance had grown to such an extent that she didn't even recognise this as a joke. 'I think he does like me!' she answered seriously, then looked up in surprise when her friends all started laughing.

She was glad to get to ballet class – she couldn't understand why her friends were acting so stupidly. Once there, however, she wished she were not. Miss Oakland was in a very bad mood. And she seemed to be picking on Cassie every few minutes. It was hard to keep her mind on the new, quite difficult syllabus for the Pre-elementary exam. *The Nutcracker* filled her thoughts.

In the end Miss Oakland confronted her.

'I'm tired of this, Cassandra. If your work doesn't improve by next week, I'm withdrawing your name from the exam list. You're just not putting enough effort in.'

Cassie apologised, but that part of her brain which was wrapped up in *The Nutcracker* went on its own sweet way, remembering, relishing every moment of her experiences at the Hippodrome.

All too soon it was the last lesson before lunch – maths. She remembered with a sickening lurch Mrs Ramsbottom's warning of the day before. Too late to do anything about it now. Perhaps she would forget?

But as soon as she set foot in the maths room, Mrs Ramsbottom pounced on her.

'May I have your work, please?'

'I'm . . . I'm sorry. I haven't had time to do it,' Cassie stuttered.

Mrs Ramsbottom's face grew dark red, with mottled patches. 'You'll hear more about this later,' she hissed, but mercifully left Cassie alone for the rest of the lesson.

By the end of the afternoon, Cassie was light-hearted again. 'You see, she didn't do anything terrible to me,' she said to Becky. 'She knows she can't, while I'm dancing Clara!'

'I shouldn't be too sure about that,' said her friend thoughtfully.

They were on their way to a jazz ballet class with the jolly Mrs Bonsing when Emily caught them up.

'Only three more performances of *Swan Lake* to go!' she said. 'I can't believe it.'

'I wonder if you'll have any more bouquets?' said Becky.

'Looks likely,' answered Emily. 'I've had one every other time.'

'And always red roses.'

'They're my favourite flowers,' said Emily.

'Did you see the flowers my aunt and uncle sent me the other night?' asked Cassie.

'Yes,' answered Becky. 'They were lovely. The room's starting to look like a florist's!'

The girls quickly peeled off their red track suits in the changing-rooms, revealing deep purple all-in-one leotards with full-length sleeves and legs. They tied the laces of their black modern dance pumps, and adjusted their pinned-up plaits.

'Another waste of time,' Cassie sighed.

'How d'you mean?' asked Emily.

'Jazz ballet,' said Cassie.

'You always used to love it!' Becky exclaimed.

'Well, I don't any more. It's got nothing to do with the great classical ballets, has it?'

Emily and Becky exchanged glances. During the lesson with Mrs Bonsing, it was obvious that Cassie's heart and mind were elsewhere. Mrs Bonsing was patient, but even she became irritated after a while.

'Cassandra,' she said quietly. 'Try to keep your mind on what we're doing. A dancer's body is only as good as the quality of her mind.'

'You don't need to tell me that,' Cassie answered quite rudely. 'I'm learning more about dancers with the Northern Ballet than I've ever done here.'

Mrs Bonsing stared at her, lost for words. Everyone in the class – except Cassie herself – knew that such rudeness to a member of staff couldn't go unheeded.

Cassie thought she was untouchable – a star in the making. Her illusion was shattered when, just after supper, she was summoned to Miss Wrench's study.

She had to sit outside for a few minutes and this gave her opportunity to reflect uncomfortably on the way she had been behaving lately. By the time she was invited into the Principal's room, she was feeling rather sick. Miss Wrench put the complaints she had received before her – mainly from Mrs Ramsbottom, Miss Oakland and Mrs Bonsing.

'Miss Oakland has reached the point of considering whether to refuse to teach you, and there is certainly doubt about your taking your first major exam.'

Cassie winced at this, but Miss Wrench went on. 'Your standards both in your dormitory and in your school work have deteriorated far below what we expect at Redwood. And, worst of all, you spoke to Mrs Bonsing in an *unforgivable* manner. Have you anything to say for yourself, Cassandra?'

'Sorry, Miss Wrench,' Cassie said in a small voice.

'Sorry isn't enough, I'm afraid.' Miss Wrench leaned across her desk, fixing her with those piercing eyes. 'I'm going to give you an ultimatum. Either your attitude at school improves one hundred per cent, or you will never be allowed to undertake another professional engagement, as long as you are a student of my school.'

Cassie looked at the Principal open-mouthed. She couldn't do that, surely? But the green eyes were unwavering in their steely gaze and Cassie knew she meant every word. She swallowed hard.

'All right, Miss Wrench, I'll try to improve.'

'Good. It's all up to you, Cassandra.'

* * *

Cassie thought about what Miss Wrench had said to her a great deal the next day. She also realised how unbearable she must have seemed to her friends, and tried to make amends. What surprised her was that they had closed in together in such a way that she was excluded. She knew it was her own fault, but it made her feel very lonely.

During a private coaching lesson with Madame Larette that evening, all her feelings came welling up and she burst into tears. Madame knew about her interview with Miss Wrench already, and talked to her gently about it. She advised Cassie to try to separate her two worlds – the world of *The Nutcracker* and the world of Redwood. While she was at school, she must only think about school matters.

'It's so hard, though,' Cassie sobbed. 'There's so much to think about.'

'You can do it!' said Madame. 'You must 'ave a good foundation in everything. And especially, you must not neglect your ballet class. Even the top artistes take their daily ballet class very seriously indeed!'

Madame's advice and Miss Wrench's ultimatum stayed with Cassie over the weeks which followed, and she made a tremendous effort with her work, both academic and dancing. Miss Oakland relented about the exam and Cassie took it the morning after a performance of *The Nutcracker*.

She was tired and, although she had worked hard recently, under the pressure of the exam, new skills started to break down and Cassie realised how under-prepared she actually was. By contrast, Emily, Abigail and Poppy seemed confident and happy when they emerged from the examination room.

'That wasn't too bad, was it?' said Abigail, smiling.

'I made a mess of the dance,' said Cassie glumly. 'And the pirouette section too.'

'Oh, don't worry,' said Emily. 'I'm sure you were fine.'

'It's quite a day for us,' said Poppy. 'Exam in the morning and last performance of *Swan Lake* tonight!'

'We ought to celebrate!' suggested Abigail.

Cassie saw her chance to win back the good opinion of her friends.

'Leave it to me,' she said. 'Becky and I will organise something for when you get back tonight.'

'Great! Thanks, Cassie,' said Abigail. 'But let's hold it in my room – it's further away from Mrs Ramsbottom.'

'What about Celia?'

'Oh, that's a point. No, it'll have to be your room then.'

Cassie and Becky spent an enjoyable lunch hour in the domestic science room. With their teacher's permission, they made some jam tarts and sweet biscuits, telling her they were going to have a little party for their friends' last performance. What they didn't tell her was that they were going to hold the party after lights out, not the next day. Mrs Eddy also gave them a bottle of lemonade and a few packets of crisps.

After supper, the two girls laid out the food invitingly in Room Twelve, and made a big notice in

133

coloured felt-tips to stick up on the wall:

WELCOME!
AND WELL DONE!
All ye little swans.

'A pity we haven't any balloons or streamers,' sighed Cassie.

'I've got some coloured sugar paper in my desk,' said Becky. 'Let's cut it into strips and make paper chains.'

Cassie's face lit up. 'That'll make it look really Christmassy for them.'

So the time up to lights out was spent happily making decorations. They dutifully got into bed at eight-thirty and switched off the light, not wanting to attract the attention of Mrs Ramsbottom. To keep each other awake, they held a whispered conversation about what Christmas presents they wanted.

'Isn't it time for them to get back yet?' asked Becky. 'We seem to have been in bed for *ages*.'

Cassie flicked her torch on to the face of her watch.

'It's ten. They won't be long now.'

In fact the girls had dozed off by the time Emily, Poppy, Abigail and Mitsi returned from the theatre, as they had stayed for a little of the last night party which the cast had thrown. The noise of their coming in woke up Cassie and Becky however, and they were able to enjoy seeing their friend's expressions of delight at the spread they had managed to lay out for them.

'This is great!' whispered Poppy. 'We didn't have time to eat much at the party at the theatre.'

'Yes, I'm ravenous,' said Abigail.

'Well, tuck in!' said Cassie happily.

They did just that, and in no time at all, the results of the baking session had disappeared.

'Well, aren't you going to tell them, Emily?' asked Poppy suddenly.

Cassie had noticed Emily wasn't saying much, but also that she looked tremendously happy. Emily smiled broadly.

'Where are the roses?' asked Mitsi.

'I put them in the sink in the bathroom,' said Emily.

'So what have you got to tell us?' whispered Cassie.

'Let me show you.' Emily crept across to the bathroom and returned, holding the bouquet of red roses she had received that night.

Cassie spotted something different right away. There was a card! She pounced on it and read:

Em, I'm so proud of you.
Your loving Dad.

Looking up, her eyes met Emily's – they were full of happy tears. Cassie gave her friend a huge hug.

'Oh, I'm so pleased for you,' she said.

'He hasn't left an address or anything,' said Emily. 'But I know he's alive and well. And it must mean he's going to make more contact soon.'

The friends chatted quietly but merrily until Abigail said she'd better get back to her room.

As she moved across to the door, she gave a start.

'What is it?' hissed Cassie.

'There was an eye looking through the key-hole!'

Cassie leaped to the door and wrenched it open. Celia was retreating down the landing.

'It was Celia,' Cassie whispered.

'Probably looking for you, Abi!'

'She won't dare tell on us, surely?' asked Abigail.

'Won't she indeed? She's done it before.'

'I'd better go quickly then,' said Abigail. 'Sorry I can't help clear up the mess.'

'That's OK,' said Cassie. 'It'll look more suspicious if you're here anyway.'

Abigail scurried off, while the room-mates fell over each other, trying to dispose of the debris of their little party as quickly as they could. They hadn't finished, however, when Mrs Ramsbottom walked in.

'So you *are* having a party!' she boomed.

'It was the last night of *Swan Lake*,' explained Emily.

'We were celebrating . . .' added Cassie lamely.

'I can see that,' said Mrs Ramsbottom. 'And what time do you think it is?'

'Eleven-thirty, Mrs Ramsbottom.'

'And what time's lights out?'

'Eight-thirty, Mrs Ramsbottom.'

'Precisely.'

'But it was a special occasion,' Cassie pleaded. 'The last time they would be little swans and—'

'I've had quite enough of little swans and Nutcrackers for one term,' Mrs Ramsbottom cut in.

Suddenly Cassie's temper got the better of her.

'And I've had enough of you! You're making our lives a misery!'

There was a dangerous silence. Through gritted teeth, Mrs Ramsbottom spoke once more.

'I'll be seeing Miss Wrench first thing in the morning. And so, no doubt, will all of you.'

12

End of Term

None of the occupants of Room Twelve had a very good night's sleep. When Cassie got out of bed, she felt as though she had been through a mill backwards.

'Well, at least Abigail got away in time,' said Emily. She looked the most cheerful of the bunch.

'I want to go home,' moaned Mitsi, who was terrified of Miss Wrench.

'Are you going home for Christmas?' asked Emily.

'No,' sighed Mitsi. 'I've got to stay at school again.' She looked very miserable at the thought.

Becky was trying, unsuccessfully, to cheer up Cassie.

'I've been rude to a teacher again,' she said heavily. 'The Wrench is bound to carry out her threat now.'

'Wait and see,' said Becky. 'We'll do our best for you.'

But Cassie couldn't honestly see what the others could do to change the Principal's mind.

They were sent for before breakfast, and trooped down to the study. The school secretary told them to sit down and wait outside as Miss Wrench was talking to a member of staff. They sat down, and it quickly became obvious which member of staff was with the Principal.

'I'd know that voice anywhere!' said Becky.

The voices from within the study became raised, particularly Mrs Ramsbottom's. The girls heard 'maths lessons', 'Swan Lake' and 'The Nutcracker' mentioned several times. There was no doubt left in their minds that she and Miss Wrench were having a row when Mrs Ramsbottom stormed out of the study, not even bothering to close the door behind her. Neither did she look at the girls, just strode straight across the hall like a guided missile.

'Wow!' muttered Becky under her breath.

The others, apart from Cassie, started to titter.

They wiped the smiles from their faces, as soon as Miss Wrench appeared in the doorway. She looked a little flustered, and there was a nervous tic in her cheek.

'Come in girls,' she said. 'And shut the door behind you.' She sat at her desk, giving herself a few moments to compose herself.

'You've been caught by your – er – housemother – having some kind of party long after lights out. This

140

is quite clearly breaking school rules and you will all be punished by a fortnight's litter duty. Don't let it happen again. You can go to breakfast now.'

The girls looked at one another as they moved towards the door. They were amazed they had got off so lightly.

'Cassandra, you can wait behind,' said Miss Wrench, with an edge to her voice.

Becky turned quickly. 'Please, Miss Wrench, don't be too hard on Cassie. She only did the party to be nice, 'cause it was their last night and everything. And I can understand why she lost her temper with Mrs Ramsbottom.'

'Oh?' said Miss Wrench, raising her eyebrows. 'Why is that, Rebecca?'

'Well, she's been picking on Cassie and the others because of them missing their maths lessons. It wasn't fair, because they couldn't help it!'

'Thank you, Rebecca,' said Miss Wrench. 'You may go.'

It was impossible to tell from the Principal's expression if what Becky had said had had any effect on her or not. Everything went quiet when Cassie's friends had left the room.

'Sit down, Cassandra,' began Miss Wrench.

'I'm *really* sorry, Miss Wrench, that I was rude to Mrs Ramsbottom. I don't know what came over me.'

'I think I gave you an ultimatum about your behaviour, earlier in the term?'

Cassie's heart sank even lower. 'Yes, Miss Wrench.'

'I really cannot countenance such rudeness to

members of staff. Is that understood?'

'Yes, Miss Wrench.'

'Another thing.' She picked up a white card from her desk and looked at it. 'I have here the result from your Pre-elementary examination.'

Cassie gasped. She hadn't been expecting this. What if she'd failed?

'You have been successful, Cassandra, but I should like to point out that you have only just scraped through, whereas several of your friends – Emily, Poppy and Abigail – have gained Honours. And Mitsuko, I believe, has been commended.'

Cassie, feeling small and disappointed, looked at her feet. It wasn't really surprising she hadn't done very well; she just hadn't worked hard enough.

'I did warn you that your attitude would have a harmful effect on your work.'

Is she going to carry out her threat? wondered Cassie. It would be dreadful never to have another opportunity like the one she had had in *The Nutcracker*.

'On the plus side,' Miss Wrench went on, 'the reports from all your other teachers have been glowing these past few weeks. It's a great pity you had to mar your record.'

Cassie couldn't speak. She was very near to tears.

'However,' said Miss Wrench, 'given the rather *peculiar* circumstances of last night's occurrence, I am not going to carry out my threat.'

'You're not?' exclaimed Cassie, her heart leaping.

'No, not *this* time. Put this behind you, and carry on the excellent work you've been doing in class.'

142

'Oh, thank you, Miss Wrench,' Cassie breathed. She ran all the way to breakfast (fortunately all the teachers were already in the dining-hall) and spilled out the good news to her friends as soon as she had found their table.

'Oh Cassie, that's great!' said Becky. 'And congratulations, Em and Poppy!'

Abigail joined the table.

'You've got Honours for your ballet exam,' Cassie blurted out.

'Oh, fantastic!' cried Abigail. 'How did you do, Cassie?'

'Oh, I just passed, but I don't mind. I'm just so happy the Wrench isn't banning me from any more theatre work.'

'I've given Celia a piece of my mind, by the way,' said Abigail. 'I'm just not having her sneaking around, spying on me.'

'I wish I could think of a good way of getting our own back,' said Poppy.

'I hardly feel cross at all with her now,' said Cassie. 'I'm just so relieved.'

'We'd better hurry up and get back to the room,' said Emily. 'There's still a load of mess to clear away before Mrs Ramsbottom's inspection.'

'Ooh yes, I'd forgotten,' said Cassie.

The girls bolted down their scrambled eggs and raced back to Room Twelve to finish tidying up. They sat on their beds and waited, but Mrs Ramsbottom didn't come.

'That's strange,' said Emily.

'I'll nip over to Lesley's. See if she's been there yet,' said Poppy.

She returned very quickly, shaking her head. 'No, they haven't been honoured with a visit.'

Emily, who was sitting in the window which overlooked the front drive, suddenly called out to her friends to come and look. They gathered round her and gazed through the smeary glass.

'It's only a taxi!' said Becky.

'Yes, but look who's heading towards it!' cried Emily.

'Mrs Ramsbottom!' they all exclaimed.

'Where d'you think she's going at this time in the morning?' asked Cassie.

'She's got her suitcases with her,' shouted Poppy excitedly.

They all stared, as the driver got out and helped stow Mrs Ramsbottom's luggage in the taxi.

'It can only mean one thing!' Cassie pronounced. 'Mrs Ramsbottom has had one row too many with the Wrench and SHE'S LEAVING!'

'Wild!' breathed Becky.

The news passed down the landing like a fireball and very soon cheering and laughter could be heard from every room. The friends rushed over to Mrs Allingham's at lunch-time to tell her all about it.

On the way, Cassie felt a sudden misgiving. 'I've had a nasty thought,' she said to Becky and Emily. 'Suppose Mrs Ramsbottom has been called away urgently to a sick relative or something? Suppose she's *coming back!*'

Emily shuddered. 'I can't bear to think that,' she said.

Mrs Allingham was inclined to think Mrs Ramsbottom had gone for good. A little bird had told her, she said, that she wasn't seeing eye to eye with Miss Wrench.

Their fears were finally put to rest by Madame Larette, who paid a surprise visit to their room that evening. She confirmed that Mrs Ramsbottom *had* gone for good, and raised an eyebrow at the broad grins which greeted this announcement.

'*Maintenant, mes chéries*, I am your new 'ousemother. At least, until Christmas.'

'Oh lovely!' burst out Cassie. She knew they would be guaranteed a happy time with Madame in charge, as she didn't care a hoot about school rules.

Madame laughed.

'But who will it be *after* Christmas, Madame?' asked Poppy.

'Miss Eiseldown wishes to resume 'er post in the new year. She 'as decided not to settle in America.'

'Oh, that's great!' cried Cassie.

'I can't believe it!' said Emily. 'Everything's turning out so well.'

'Let's 'ope it stays that way,' said Madame. 'I wanted to talk to you about a little demonstration of your work I'm planning for the last day of term. For your parents and families.'

'Is that instead of a proper show?' asked Emily.

'Yes, with so many of you missing, we didn't think it was worth attempting a full-scale show.'

'Are we doing class work then?' asked Cassie.

'Yes, I thought we would do a sample ballet class. I think many of the parents would find that very interesting. But also, I would like to show off my little swans in their beautiful costumes.'

Emily smiled happily at Mitsi and Poppy. Cassie couldn't help feeling that old left-out feeling, as she knew there was nothing from *The Nutcracker* she could dance as a solo.

'And 'ow about one of your lovely traditional Japanese dances, Mitsuko?'

'Oh, yes, Madame,' Mitsi agreed, her eyes shining. 'I'll ask my mother to send a costume right away.'

'Thank you, Mitsuko. That will be *très charmant*.'

She turned to Cassie, her eyes twinkling. 'I 'aven't forgotten you, Cassandra. I'd like to teach you a short solo, in the character of Clara, to some of *The Nutcracker* music – perhaps the Transformation Scene.'

'Oh, wonderful!' cried Cassie. 'I could wear my nightdress.'

'Well now,' said Madame, patting her bun, 'I must do my rounds and be a good 'ousemother. *Au revoir*.'

'Good night, Madame,' they all called, bobbing curtsys as she left the room.

The last couple of weeks of the Christmas term flew by. There was preparation for the demonstration and also quite a lot of work in their school subjects, finishing off various topics. They were busy too in art and craft, making decorations to festoon the hall and classrooms.

When the last day of term arrived, everything and everyone was ready for the displays of work in all subjects. Everyone, that is, except Mitsi. She was terribly upset, and Cassie and the others were having a very hard time trying to keep her calm.

'I can't believe that Mum has forgotten to send it!' she moaned.

'Don't be silly, Mitsi,' said Becky. 'She won't have forgotten to send your costume. It must have got delayed in the post, that's all. You know what it's like near Christmas.'

'Well, that doesn't help,' said Mitsi. 'I still haven't got a costume.'

'You'll still dance beautifully just in your leotard,' Cassie said reassuringly.

'It won't be the same at all!' Mitsi wailed. 'It won't be authentic. If my father were here, he'd be *horrified*.'

'But he won't be here to see,' said Cassie, promptly wishing she hadn't.

'No, worse luck,' said Mitsi miserably. 'And I'm here for Christmas, without my family.'

'Well, it'll be so much nicer with Madame than with Mrs Ramsbottom. Just think of that!' said Cassie. But Mitsi had burst into tears.

'Come on, let's go and put the finishing touches to our art displays,' said Becky, anxious to change the subject. But even in the art room, Mitsi returned to her theme.

'It's going to be awful being stuck here again all holiday, especially at *Christmas*!' she said.

'Don't forget you've got me!' said Poppy brightly.

147

'And me!' added Cassie. She would have to stay on at school for part of the holiday, until the run of *The Nutcracker* had finished. Her last performance was to be on Christmas Eve, and so, fortunately, she would be back with her family by Christmas Day. She was quite looking forward to the experience of being at Redwood with just Poppy and Mitsi and one or two teachers, but realised that Mitsi could make everything quite difficult if she went on like this.

'We'll have a great time with the school to ourselves,' Cassie said. 'And Mum said you and Poppy could come home with me for Christmas Day and Boxing Day.'

'That's really nice of her!' said Poppy.

'Yes, thank her for me,' said Mitsi stiffly, without a flicker of pleasure in her eyes.

Cassie sighed. Unlike all the other children she had met at Redwood, Mitsi's homesickness seemed to be getting worse, not better, as time went on. Cassie's thoughts flitted to the demonstration they would be giving that afternoon. If only Mitsi's costume would arrive by second post – that would cheer her a little. It still wasn't the same as having her parents there, though. Cassie's own parents were coming. They came to everything. They had loved seeing her in *The Nutcracker* and they would be watching it again on Christmas Eve, and driving her and her friends home after the performance.

She knew she would feel sad when she took off her Clara costume for the last time. It had been such a wonderful experience, dancing with Northern Ballet.

And she had learned such a tremendous amount! More than anything, it had given her the confidence to feel that she really could become a professional dancer when she grew up. Anton Redowsky had more or less told her so. He had said she showed lots of potential, lots of promise and must work very hard to realise her ambitions.

'One day,' he told her, 'we shall be zeeing your name at ze front of ze theatre, in *Giselle* or *Swan Lake*!'

Cassie smiled to herself at the memory. She would miss Anton, and the children in the cast she had got to know. But that's what it was like in the theatre – you always had to move on to new challenges, new people. She was glad that so far she had been able to keep her school-friends, Becky and Emily.

As if guessing her thought, Becky squeezed her arm at that moment. 'Time for lunch, Cassie,' she said. 'Then we've got to get ready for this silly demonstration. Thank goodness I'm only in the class work section!'

The girls called in at the secretary's office to see if there had been a last-minute delivery of Mitsi's longed-for parcel, but there hadn't.

'Oh, what shall I do?' cried Mitsi, wringing her hands.

Cassie and the others guided her back to Room Twelve after lunch, and tried to interest her in getting her little swan costume ready to take to the studio changing-rooms.

'It's horrible we've got to give these back to the Birmingham Royal Ballet wardrobe today,' said Emily, smoothing down the white net of her ballet dress on its coat-hanger. 'Oh, I can't wait to show Mum my bouquet and the card from Dad!'

Cassie wondered to herself if Mrs Pickering would have such a happy reaction to them as Emily. You could never tell with grown-ups. And, after all, Emily's dad still hadn't left an address or phone number. But she kept her thoughts to herself, praying that nothing would shatter Emily's hopes.

There was a knock on the door.

'Come in!' called Emily, who happened to be the nearest.

The door opened and Mitsi's mother walked in, holding a large box.

'Your costume!' she said, handing it to Mitsi, who couldn't speak at first for shock. Then she recovered herself and threw herself at her mother.

'Oh, Mitsuko,' said her mother. 'I could tell from your letter how much you were missing us!'

'You can see my solo now,' said Mitsi excitedly. 'And our little swans' dance. Just in time, before the costumes have to go back!'

'Yes, I'm so glad I flew over. It's lovely to be with you, darling.'

Mitsi clung to her mother again, sobbing uncontrollably, and the friends thought it best to gather up their costumes and leave the two of them together in private.

'Oh, I'm ever so glad Mitsi's mum has come!' said Cassie in the changing-rooms.

'What's that?' asked Abigail, joining the group of

friends. 'Did you say Mitsi's mum?'

'Yes, she's flown from Japan to see Mitsi's solo. And she's brought her the traditional Japanese costume.'

'Oh, thank goodness,' said Abigail.

There was a wail from the other end of the changing-room. It was Celia.

'I can't find *any* of my pink leotards,' she shouted. 'Has anyone seen them? Miss Oakland will *kill* me!'

Cassie looked thoughtfully at Abigail. 'Anything to do with you?' she whispered.

'Who, me?' said Abigail, grinning. 'Cassie, how could you think such a thing!'

The demonstration went off smoothly and successfully. Abigail relented and gave Celia her leotards back at the last minute, and of course, Mitsi had her wonderful, brilliantly-coloured satin costume in which to dance her solo. Cassie's own solo was 'a picture' according to Mrs Allingham, who was in the audience. She hadn't been able to get to the theatre to see *The Nutcracker* or *Swan Lake*, so she was very pleased to watch her young friends give a sample of what they had been up to at the Hippodrome. When Joy and Jake Brown congratulated their daughter on her solo, Cassie thought how strange it was that she wouldn't be going back home with them for the start of the holiday. The thought of staying on in an empty school suddenly felt a lot less appealing.

'See you on Christmas Eve, Mum,' she said, giving Joy a hug.

'Yes, darling. Good luck with your last two performances. And give the last one everything you've got, 'cause we'll be watching!'

She paused and looked round. 'Now which are your new friends who are coming back with us over Christmas?'

'This is Poppy, Mum. And Mitsi's over there with her mother, talking to Madame.'

While Joy was getting to know Poppy, Mitsi and her mum moved over to their group.

'Mitsi will be very welcome at Christmas,' Joy said to Mrs Fujiwara.

'Oh, that's so kind of you, but it will no longer be necessary.'

Cassie looked into Mitsi's shining eyes and thought she could guess what was coming next.

'I shall be taking Mitsuko home with me tomorrow,' explained Mrs Fujiwara. 'We have decided to take her away from ballet school and bring her back to Japan.'

'And Dad's going to teach me all his dances,' broke in Mitsi. 'And I can live at home!'

There was consternation for a few minutes, when the room-mates realised that they were seeing Mitsi for the very last time. After a lot of hugs and a few tears, Mitsi invited each of her friends to come and spend a holiday in Japan if ever they wanted to. Mrs Fujiwara cuddled her daughter and smiled at Joy Brown.

'I didn't realise she was so homesick, until I had a letter from her a fortnight ago. Children need the support of their families, don't you think, Mrs Brown?'

'Yes indeed,' said Joy, uncomfortably aware that Poppy was standing beside her.

'Keep in touch, Mitsi, won't you?' said Cassie. 'I like writing letters.'

'Oh, good,' said Mitsi. 'It'll be great to keep up with all the ballet school gossip. From a distance!'

Everyone laughed. Cassie put an arm round Poppy's shoulder.

'Well, looks like it's just going to be me and you sticking around.'

'I don't mind,' whispered Poppy, with a glint in her green eyes. 'Just think of the mischief we can get up to while the Wrench is away!'

Cassie began to think it would be fun staying at school after all. And, once *The Nutcracker* was over, she and Poppy would be able to have a terrific Christmas together, in the Brown household.

She looked around at her room-mates and was filled with a warm Christmassy feeling. Life at Redwood could sometimes be tough, but friends, old and new, made all the difference. She gave a last wave to Mitsi.

'Don't forget us, Mitsi,' she called. 'Your friends at the ballet school!'

'I'll never forget you!' Mitsi called back. 'Never!'